A JOURNEY THROUGH

Corinthians

WITH KIM JAGGERS

ISBN 979-8-218-21681-8

First paperback edition, June 2023

Edited by Elissa Cox

Cover and Interior Design by Stephanie Anfinson

acknowledgments

I am so thankful for so many who encouraged me to put this book together. I don't think it would have come about except for the prodding, prayers, and encouragement of those who study the Word with me in the early mornings via my social media posts. Many mornings, I rub my tired eyes but joyfully study extra hard because I know God will help us encourage one another day after day. Thank you, friends, for being iron sharpening iron and pouring into this. I am also incredibly thankful for Elissa Cox, who, while washing dishes one morning, felt the Lord clearly lay on her heart to reach out to lend her editing skills to help me with this book. And I definitely needed lots of help! Elissa's ideas have gone far beyond grammar corrections, and her love for Jesus is real. Elissa also connected me to the gifted and sweet Stephanie Anfinson, who used her graphic design skills to birth this beautiful book. As always, I appreciate my family who graciously sees themselves directly and indirectly in the stories I tell and still encourages me to keep on writing and sharing about our daily walk together toward our eternal home. And when I think about home, I think about my friend Karen Alexander Doyel who is there in Heaven—how she inspired and challenged me and many others to "love Jesus more tomorrow than we do today." May this book help us to do just that . . . because what a Savior He is! What a King we serve! What hope we have for all our tomorrows when we know Him in a real, daily relationship! Thank you, Jesus, for all you've done and continue to do. May this book honor and glorify You alone!

first
corinthians

first corinthians

INTRODUCTION

Life had been emotional and hard when the Lord brought me back to Paul's letters to the Corinthians. Having just finished Romans, I opened to Paul's first letter to the church at Corinth as life handed me a plate full of emotions.

I had exhausted myself physically, preparing for a big college graduation party for my son Ben. I had been fighting back tears over him growing up when our precious chocolate lab, Braylee, died unexpectedly. I was devastated but had to try to pull it together, even as I watched both my grown sons cry like babies. While all this happened, our business continued to be busy and stressful; and I was having trouble sleeping.

Life
Trouble
Problems
Pain

We all face these times, and when we do, if we are honest, we often ask ourselves, "Do I truly trust God to 'sustain me to the end?'" (1 Cor. 1:8)

I read that verse, and all the "buts" began to roll through my mind: "But my kids are growing up. But my sweet dog died. But my friend is sick with cancer. But my business is stressful. But my parents are aging. But my country seems crazy."

After all these years of reading the Bible, going to church, praying, and seeing God be so very faithful, do I sometimes doubt that He will still sustain me? Yes, if I'm honest. And when I doubt, am I tempted to go my own way? Yes, I still am.

Just like those Corinthian Christians who were going their own way, I am still tempted to doubt God and allow sin to creep into my life when it gets hard.

Are you?

And when life gets difficult—when you feel tired, sad, mistreated, or (a big one for me) unappreciated—do you almost feel as if you are allowed a few sin passes? Just between us, has this ridiculous thought crossed your mind? It has mine. You know, maybe just a few "comfort sins" will ease the pain. Perhaps some complaining will make me feel better, like, "I have the right to be irritable. My house is a mess. My work is incredibly busy. It seems I'm always helping others, and no one wants to help me." And on and on . . .

It is easy to get off track and spiral down instead of remembering that God, through Paul, reminds us we have everything we need in Jesus.

But does God really mean everything?

I am convinced that when we turn away from our emotions and look to the Word, we can't help but know God means absolutely everything.

Everything
Always
In Jesus

Yes, God means everything—even when you're tired, even when your job stinks, even when your kids grow up, even when your dog dies, even when your spouse isn't helping enough, even when you don't have a spouse to help, even when your heart is breaking over your prodigal, even when your health is failing, even when everyone else seems to have an easier life than you.

God will still sustain you to the end! He says so in His Word!

Friends, we must be sensitive to God's voice, even—and especially—when life is hard and we are tempted to believe we have the right to ignore Him or go our own way and sin.

But when we remember His faithfulness and keep following Him through sadness, pain, and stress, we get the best comfort of all. We get a keen sense of His abiding, sustaining presence—God with us!

As Paul Tripp says, "When we remember God has an amazing, glorious future planned for His children, we won't live like this moment is all we have." And that perspective, rather than running to some comfort sin, reminds us God will sustain us to the end; it brings true peace and refreshing hope!

Oh, let's read Corinthians together!

Thousands of years later,

this letter to the Corinthians,

these holy words you can now
hold in your hands, are also
aimed at our hearts

for our good

and God's glory!

1 *day one*

For 18 months, the Apostle Paul had made tents during the week in Corinth and preached every Sabbath. The Jews had, for the most part, rejected the Gospel, and most who came to believe in the Messiah as "the Jew of Jews" were Gentiles. (That's a whole other story, but let's move on for now.)

Paul then left the young church in the hands of his faithful friends Aquila and Priscilla and continued his missionary journeys—and four years passed.

While ministering in Ephesus, Paul received two letters about his beloved church in Corinth. Those he had preached to and prayed with were fighting with each other and not fighting sin.

And Paul's head must have dropped with disappointment and discouragement.

He had taught with all he had. He had seen genuine conversion and true faith birthed. Dead men had come alive, but now the young church was full of division and immorality.

Corinth was a dark place.

Evil forces were at work.

The young church was in danger of falling away.

So Paul picked up his pen—inspired by a merciful and righteous God—to plead with those true believers who had compromised with sin to walk back to truth and come together in unity for their good and God's glory.

And thousands of years later, this letter to the Corinthians, these holy words you can now hold in your hands, are also aimed at our hearts for our good and God's glory! Oh, aren't you excited to pick up this letter? It is no accident, you know. For the Lord of Lords, who gloriously orchestrates all things, has guided your eyes to these words for this time! May He give you ears to hear and eyes to see just what He wants you to see and hear! For His words are better than anything I could ever write.

Please pray and read 1 Corinthians Chapter 1.

2 *day two*

Please pray and reread 1 Corinthians Chapter 1.

I wonder if A. W. Tozer had just read Paul's words to the Corinthians as he beckoned his generation to stand up for truth in an immoral culture when he said, "Another kind of religious leader must rise among us. He must be of the old prophet type, a man who has seen visions of God and has heard a voice from the Throne. When he comes (and I pray there will be not one but many), he will stand in flat contradiction to everything our smirking, smooth civilization holds dear."

I wonder if any of us hear that same call today as we look at our world, our churches, our friends, and maybe even our own families.

The Apostle Paul wasted no time as he began his letter by reminding those who were fighting with each other and living just like the lost in their culture that they had all they needed in Jesus to live better—in unity with each other and for the cause of Christ. (1 Cor. 1:4–9)

Paul was quick to tell them that it wasn't by human words of eloquent wisdom that he wrote to them but by the power of the Cross alone. (1 Cor. 1:7) That same power, he said, was available to them. (See Romans 6 and Ephesians 1.)

No, seriously, please read those passages.

Paul knew the power of the Cross and desperately wanted those early believers (and us) to remember that power. He knew his life had been wonderfully and radically changed by the power of Christ alone.

And with that, let's also understand that what Paul saw all around him is what we are still very much seeing today:

11

> **"The word of the cross is folly to those who are perishing, but to those who are being saved it is the power of God." (1 Cor. 1:18)**

Yes, our smirking, smooth, politically correct society mocks Christianity like never before. Like Tozer and Paul, we see it. We feel it. Like Tozer, Paul was (and is) beckoning a world-compromising, divided Church to bravely remember the power of the Cross and to understand their calling. He was imploring them to choose differently.

Paul is also talking to all of us who call Jesus Lord:

> **"For consider your calling, brothers: not many of you were wise according to worldly standards, not many were powerful, not many were of noble birth. But God chose what is foolish in the world to shame the wise; God chose what is weak in the world to shame the strong; God chose what is low and despised in the world, even things that are not, to bring to nothing things that are, so that no human being might boast in the presence of God. And because of him you are in Christ Jesus, who became to us wisdom from God, righteousness and sanctification and redemption, so that, as it is written, 'Let the one who boasts, boast in the Lord.'" (1 Cor. 1:26–31)**

Friend, you may feel low, like a nobody; you may be called foolish, weak, and powerless; and you may very well be despised by this world—and if so, good!

Why good? Good, because that's exactly who God uses to boast in the power of the Cross!

Oh, friend, may those who have tasted the goodness of the Lord, may those who were broken and made whole, and may those who were dead and made alive by the power of the Cross boast alone in the Savior who has set us free!

Yes, may we remember in this day—in this culture that we are living in—that in Christ alone, we have all we need!

And as we remember, may we boldly choose to follow Him, even when others do not, and may we sacrificially love others so a lost world might want what we have and give glory to our Savior alone.

What a Savior He is! All glory, honor, and power to Him alone!

Why not spend a few minutes today praising the Lord for what He has done in your life? Will you get a pen and paper and write some of these things down? Perhaps, make a list on your phone, and add to it throughout the day. When we slow down and think of it, we have so very much to thank Him for!

3 *day three*

Please pray and read 1 Corinthians Chapter 2.

I'm not sure if anything comes as close to rattling my faith as when godly people walk away from Jesus and do ungodly things, and this was exactly the news Paul had received about the church in Corinth.

We see it today as many continue to choose the praise of men, compromising with the world instead of clinging to truth and living for the praise of God. Just turn on the news, or look at social media. It is disheartening, isn't it?

Paul reminded those in Corinth—and us today—that their faith could never rest in the wisdom of men but only in the power of God. He wrote:

> **"For I decided to know nothing among you except Jesus Christ and him crucified . . . so that your faith might not rest in the wisdom of men but in the power of God." (2 Cor. 2:2, 5)**

Oh, friend, let's remind our weary selves that our eyes and our hearts can only ever count on one object of perfection—and that is Jesus Christ.

Every person on the planet is capable of failing. That means you, and that means me—and even those in our churches and those on stages whom we've come to admire.

We can't ever put our faith in the flesh. But we can learn to better listen to the Holy Spirit inside each of us as believers.

The Apostle Paul was pleading with those Corinthian believers to keep their eyes on Jesus in the midst of the immorality around them, heed the voice of the Holy Spirit inside them, and remember they have the mind of Christ to instruct them.

Open your Bible, and read 1 Corinthians 2:9–15. Those precious, holy words were written for their hearts then and our hearts today. It is no accident that God has you reading them right now. Yes, those God-inspired words are better than any human pen will ever compose, tweet, or post. And just when you need them, the Holy Spirit will remind you what God says in His Word.

The time you spend in God's Word will always be well spent. If you can't find time to open the Word, friend, you need to adjust your priorities and your schedule.

Why? Because you can count on this: this world can be hard, and the truth will be twisted. The world, and sometimes those in the church, will run 100 mph the wrong way. But we can know the way to take because we have available the mind of Christ in God's Word. (1 Cor. 1:16) That Word will be folly to the world and even twisted by some in ministry. (1 Cor. 1:14)

Yet the spiritual person judges all things by the Word and listens intently—above all the noise—for the Holy Spirit's guidance so they might interpret spiritual truths and walk out their faith well—loving Jesus and others around them. (1 Cor. 1:13)

> **"No eye has seen, no ear has heard, and no mind has imagined what God has prepared for those who love him." (1 Cor. 2:9 NLT)**

No eye
No ear
No mind

You can't even imagine what God has planned! Hang on! Keep listening! Keep following! Keep loving Him! What a Savior!

4 *day four*

Please pray and read 1 Corinthians 3:1–15.

They were sitting in church but looked just like those in the world around them. They probably raised their hands on the Sabbath after raising their glasses in a drunken stupor the night before.

Paul absolutely loved those people, but he called the believers "carnal" and said he had to feed them as "babes in Christ" with milk because they couldn't handle solid spiritual food. (1 Cor. 3:1–3)

Their lives were characterized by envy, strife, and division. They identified themselves as followers of human teachers rather than simply followers of Christ. (1 Cor. 3:4)

Today, believers like them might follow the coolest pastor on Twitter and occasionally tune in to a podcast, but they likely rarely soberly read the Word and allow that solid, spiritual food to change their behavior and cause real growth in their lives. These are baby believers who have no spiritual muscle. They are weak when it comes to sin, and their lives look almost like the lost among them.

When hard times come, they fall apart, and some walk away.

Paul was talking to the mature and the immature believers when he said that one day, all of our works will be tested by fire—some will receive a reward, and some will suffer loss. (1 Cor. 3:13–14)

And we can't skip past those words.

None of us

We must pause and ask God to show us the truth about the lives we are living.

Can others tell we love Jesus?

Are we choosing to follow Christ above all and storing up treasure in Heaven, or are we spending all our time living for ourselves and looking just like the lost world around us?

This question is worth some time. So why not look at your time? Pull out your calendar; look at your week and your past weeks. Think about where you spend your time. Ponder what you think about. What consumes you?

Are you concerned about the cause of Christ? Do you want others around you to know Him and walk in freedom?

Are you convinced that serving Him is where you will find your true joy? Or are you only chasing temporary things that can never bring lasting joy?

These are questions to ask yourself. These are questions I ask myself again and again because we can all get distracted.

But when we turn our eyes to Jesus and walk on mission with Him, what an adventure we will have—what delight! What a reward to see Jesus at work in and through us!

Spend some time asking the Lord to help you prioritize your time as He would have you.

5 *day five*

Please pray and read 1 Corinthians 3:16–17.

And then . . . Paul wrote more hard, true words to every believer:

> **"Do you not know that you are the temple of God and that the Spirit of God dwells in you?" (1 Cor. 3:16 NKJV)**

As a Christian, the Holy Spirit lives inside of *you* right now.

Right now

The Holy Spirit is inside of *you*!

Does this not blow you away? It is supernatural! My mind can hardly fathom the magnitude of this truth. But the question is not, how can we explain this? The question is, what are we doing with this fact?

Are you hearing God's voice? What does your life involve Him in? Are those good things or things you'd rather no one see?

But hold on. Prepare yourself. Paul continued:

> **"If anyone defiles the temple of God, God will destroy him. For the temple of God is holy, which temple you are." (1 Cor. 3:17 NKJV)**

The temple of God is holy. And *you* are that temple.

And if anyone defiles the temple of God, God will destroy him.

Woe, those aren't fluffy, feel-good, prosperity-preaching words. They are sobering words, and they are true. And these words should impact each of us and affect how we live each day.

This day
Really

If we read the Bible and do not apply it to our lives, we are just hearers of the Word. We know our Lord's brother James warned us that if we do this, we are deceiving ourselves. (James 1:22)

> **"But the one who looks into the perfect law, the law of liberty, and perseveres, being no hearer who forgets but a doer who acts, he will be blessed in his doing." (James 1:25)**

Blessed

Oh, friend, may we grow up in Christ. May we allow God's Word to "read us" and change how we live. And when we do, may we find strength for each new day, purpose far beyond any earthly passion, and joy far greater than anything this temporary world has to offer!

Oh, what a Savior!

6 *day six*

Please pray and read 1 Corinthians 3:18–23.

As Christians, we so want what we believe to be good, right, and true to be embraced by our culture. We often find ourselves exuberantly cheering the slightest hint of Christianity in our political figures when they use a Bible verse in their speech or our athletes when they thank God after a victory.

Sometimes our motives are pure, hoping that person truly knows the Savior.

Other times, when we check our hearts, we realize we just want what we consider true to be acclaimed as wise by the world.

But we know that the wisdom of God is foolishness to most people. Rarely is godly truth celebrated in our culture. The sad fact is that we are seeing the things of God increasingly mocked and violence perpetuated against Christianity in record numbers around the world.

But remember, what the world celebrates and calls wise is folly to God. And He is always correct in His assessment:

> **"Let no one deceive himself. If anyone among you thinks that he is wise in this age, let him become a fool that he may become wise." (1 Cor. 3:18)**

So let's face it: at some point in your walk with the Lord, the world will call you foolish. And that's okay.

> **"For the wisdom of this world is folly with God. For it is written, 'He catches the wise in their craftiness,' and again, 'The Lord knows the thoughts of the wise, that they are futile.' So let no one boast in men. For all things are yours . . ."**
> **(1 Cor. 3:19–21)**

God reminds His children to keep this perspective as the world mocks:

> **"For all things are yours, whether Paul or Apollos or Cephas or the world or life or death or the present or the future—all are yours, and you are Christ's, and Christ is God's." (1 Cor. 3:21b–23)**

Regardless of how the world sees our faith, we can confidently walk forward, remembering that because of Jesus, we have all we need. Wisdom is in Him, whether the world around us recognizes it or not.

Our strength comes from Him.

Our security rests in Him.

Our hope is always in Him.

In Him

And any truly praiseworthy thing we will ever do will come from the overflow of the time we spend at His feet. Oh, friend, again today, take your eyes off the world. Lay down your need to be praised by others, and run to Him over and over. It's there that you'll have all you will ever need.

Hold on to this truth today. Ask the Lord to remind you of it. Write this on a card, and stick it on your mirror if you need to do so:

> **"But seek first the kingdom of God and his righteousness, and all these things will be added to you." (Matt. 6:33)**

7 *day seven*

Please pray and read 1 Corinthians Chapter 4.

Paul had just finished telling the Corinthian believers—living in the midst of a very ungodly culture—that they had all they needed in Jesus. (1 Cor. 3)

Then he said, "So, go do whatever you want. Live like you want, do what feels right, and make yourself happy. You have your get-out-of-hell card. Be you. Be free to do what feels right to you!"

No, he didn't!

But that's exactly how some of them were living. Their lives looked just like the culture around them. They had forgotten who they were. They had forgotten they had been bought with the highest price and were to live with a purpose.

In 1 Corinthians 4, Paul reminded them who they were. Those who trust Jesus for salvation are servants of Christ and stewards of the mysteries of God. (1 Cor. 4:1)

As a child of God, you are trusted to steward the mysteries of God. As you sit at His feet, He will reveal the deep things of Himself to you. (Look back at 1 Cor. 2:10.) And because so great a gift has been given to you—the mind of Christ revealed to you through His Word—Paul said it is required of stewards to be found faithful. (1 Cor. 4:2)

Faithfulness is required—not suggested.

And we who have been bought with the same precious blood as those believers who first read this letter must also remember that.

Faithfulness is required immediately of all who call Jesus Lord, not when we get done being young and/or having fun.

It is required regardless of what others around us choose to do.

We need to remember who we are and do what we are called to do.

It seems many Christians today do one of two things: join in the sin around them, like those Corinthians, or pull away from the lost and shut themselves off entirely in "holy huddles."

But we are called to live faithful to our King in this world—among the lost—and steward this "mystery of God" well so others can see Jesus and give Him glory.

If we aren't faithful, we have absolutely no chance of doing that.

And if we live our lives cocooned from the rest of the world or as "closet Christians," we aren't stewarding the mystery of God well either.

Yes, the world we live in scoffs and scorns, but we aren't tasked with changing the culture. We are simply called to live as faithful servants to our King so those around us—those at work, those at school, those in our neighborhoods—might see Him in us and want what we have.

As our eyes stay fixed on our Savior, day in and day out, and as we faithfully follow Him and love those who don't know Him—and even those who mock Him—others will see something different in us, whether they know what it is or not.

They will be drawn to this mystery!

And as we are faithful by stewarding this glorious "mystery" well, the Kingdom of God powerfully advances.

One life at a time, one heart impacting another, is the very best way to change the culture—much more than any political effort will ever yield.

And even better, it is the best way to help someone find Jesus so that what really matters—their eternity—will be forever changed.

Remember who you are! Remember, servant of the Most High God, that you've been bought with the highest price. Be faithful, and steward this glorious mystery of God well! And others will see Him in you!

Spend some time praying today about how you might steward well what you have been shown. Ask the Lord to open your eyes to those opportunities to allow the mysteries He has revealed to you to be evident in your life in a way others will notice.

Any truly praiseworthy thing we will ever do will come from the overflow of the time we spend at His feet.

8 *day eight*

Please pray and reread 1 Corinthians 4:1–5.

Remember, Paul knew what was going on in that messed up church he had left four years prior.

They were fighting with each other. They were getting drunk. They were sexually immoral. One guy was sleeping with his father's wife. Everyone knew it, and no one confronted him.

But Paul waited to mention all this in his letter to the wayward church at Corinth.

Instead, Paul first spent time appealing to them to remember what Jesus did for them and who they were—servants of Christ. They were to be faithful and steward the mysteries of God well. (1 Cor. 4:1–2)

And then Paul threw in a couple of sentences that, at first glance, seem out of place. But these words were strategically placed by Paul's pen—through God's inspiration—because he knew very well the argument the enemy would use:

> **"It is of little importance to me that I should be judged by you or by any human court. In fact, I don't even judge myself. For I am not conscious of anything against myself, but I am not justified by this. It is the Lord who judges me."** **(1 Cor. 4:3–4 CSB)**

Paul told them upfront that it doesn't matter what others think or even what they themselves think; it only matters what God thinks.

Paul's pen became a sword preemptively squashing the enemy's argument (still in use today) that excuses sin based on what others are doing in our culture, or opinion polls, or what seems right to our human emotions.

Paul pointed those who read his letter to the unchanging, perfect truth of God. He based all he said and did on that fact, and with confidence, Paul said:

> **"It is the Lord who judges me." (1 Cor. 4:4)**

Because Paul believed it only matters what God thinks, Paul was confident to speak freedom-giving truth that may very well have upset his readers because he was free from the need to please men. Paul boldly lived his life for the Lord because he knew how he lived would be judged by God—as will the life of every believer.

One day, all Christians will stand before the Lord and give an account of how we have stewarded this great gift of life we have been given. Paul talked about this "judgment seat of Christ" when he said:

> **"For we must all appear before the judgment seat of Christ, so that each may be repaid for what he has done in the body, whether good or evil." (2 Cor. 5:10)**

This is a tremendously sobering thought; God's Word also says:

> **"For nothing is secret that will not be revealed, nor anything hidden that will not be known and come to light." (Luke 8:17 NKJV)**

So what do we do with *that*?

We better pay close attention and resolve to keep our eyes on Jesus—because that's where the hope is! This Jesus who died for us is the One who loves us with an unending, perfect love. He knows everything we have ever done and will ever do, yet He still chose to die for us. He calls us the apple of His eye. He is all good. He knows every day we will ever live. We can trust Him more than we trust ourselves.

When we think about all this, surely our hearts know it is for our good to follow Him. But do our hearts *really* know this?

Most believers I know will tell you they don't fear physical death because they know they will be with Jesus in the blink of an eye. Believers know God sent His Son to die in our place. This death defeated the devil and forever released us from the fear of earthly death. (Heb. 2:9, 15)

Yes, it's true that we who trust Jesus need no longer fear our own physical death. But we can sure fear other kinds of deaths—the death of our finances, the death of our comforts, the death of our reputations, the death of our relationships, and on and on.

Oh, we know that when we die physically, we will be with Jesus, but if those other things—the things we look to for our security—were to die this side of Heaven, we question if God would be with us then.

The enemy continually tries to use these fears to convince us that God, who sent His Son to die for us, will somehow be absent and uninvolved in the hard things we might face in this life.

And it is there, in that fear, that we often decide to take things into our own hands and sin.

We know the Bible tells us that Jesus is a merciful and faithful High Priest who has suffered and been tempted and is able to give aid to those who are tempted. (Heb. 2:17–18)

Jesus understands that we are tempted to fear and worry and fret. He knows we sometimes place our security in temporary things instead of in Him. He knows we are tempted to think God doesn't love us when we find our circumstances difficult.

But even when we "think wrong," Jesus doesn't walk away.

Jesus is a sympathetic mediator between God and us. He knows what the enemy is throwing at us. He understands our weaknesses.

He is there on the throne, talking to the Father about you! What a *great mystery* this is to steward and carry with you!

Paul David Tripp asserts that many of us just want the "Prozac Jesus," who will simply make us feel better. But the truth is that God is after so much more in His temples of His Holy Spirit—all believers. He wants to give us *real freedom* that we can walk in and that others will be drawn to!

The Apostle Paul knew God could take hard things and cause us to love Him more, love others better, and advance His Kingdom. Paul wanted those Corinthians to know this, and he wants us to know this.

Oh, friend, God is at work for so much more than our temporary happiness. He is patiently and powerfully at work for our holiness. We owe our precious Savior our obedience, but don't miss how incredibly freeing it is to follow Jesus and live for an audience of One—as Paul was doing when he wrote this letter! When we let God be our Guide above all else, we will be free from the misery of living for the fickle, never-satisfied praise of others!

Oh, may our hearts be reminded of this:

> **"Therefore judge nothing before the time, until the Lord comes, who will both bring to light the hidden things of darkness and reveal the counsels of the hearts. Then each one's praise will come from God." (1 Cor. 4:5 NKJV)**

And that's no small thing!

God's Word is so good! And this letter is just getting started!

9 *day nine*

Let's take a pause.

Yesterday, I talked about fear and worry, and there are so many things in this world right now that tempt us to fear.

I'm sick of seeing the enemy rob us of peace because we are distracted, discouraged, and gripped by fear. The enemy really uses that.

But here's one thing I've learned that has disarmed him time and time again in my life: when I hear the enemy telling me all the bad things that could happen—the "what-ifs"—I've learned to say "*even if.*"

Even if the worst nightmare or scenario the evil one can throw at me comes true—even if *that* happens:

- God is still good. (Exod. 34:6)
- God is still faithful. (2 Thess. 3:3)
- God will not leave me. (Deut. 31:6)
- God can receive glory, even through that hard thing. (Rom. 8:28)

I've learned to let my mind temporarily go to the worst-case scenario by saying, "Even if that happens, the above is still true."

This disarms the enemy.

As I do this, I have learned to enjoy my blessings instead of being gripped by the fear of losing them or that I won't get others.

Friend, let's not be afraid to possess the land God is giving us because of the giants we worry might be there. (Numbers 14)

Let's remember the truth. Let's help each other walk past the lies and fear and remember that our eternity is secure! God has great plans for us! Nothing can change that! (John 10:28)

One day, one glorious day, our faith will become sight. And all the hard things that happen, or that we worry might happen, will be no more.

But until then, let's walk in truth—fear-killing, joy-bringing, peace-giving truth!

Yes, God is still good. He is still faithful. He will not leave us. He can receive glory, even through hard things.

So let's not give in to fear but walk forward and really enjoy the blessings of this day.

10 *day ten*

Please pray and reread 1 Corinthians 4:6–21.

They had believed in Jesus as their Savior, but they were still looking to this world to make them happy—and were making a mess of things. They were fighting with each other, looking for love in all the wrong places, and seeking to be filled with the fleeting things of this world.

Like many Christians, they were searching for something they already had.

Like us, the Corinthians lived in a world that placed great value on temporary things, and they were falling into the temptation to be like the world around them.

Paul told those baby believers at Corinth:

> **"You are already full! You are already rich!" (1 Cor. 4:8a NKJV)**

Paul then contrasted what he faced as an apostle—condemnation, ridicule, hunger, thirst, poverty, beatings, homelessness, and persecution—to the relatively easy life they were living in Corinth as Christians. (1 Cor. 4:8–13)

Then Paul said, you need to "imitate me." (1 Cor. 4:16 NKJV)

That was surely a hard sell!

Those weren't seeker-friendly, fill-the-pew kinds of words.

Why would Paul say such a thing?

Wouldn't he sell more books if he encouraged them that they could live their best lives now?

Then, with all the spunk his pen could muster, he said:

> **"What do you want? Shall I come to you with a rod, or in love and a spirit of gentleness?" (1 Cor. 4:21 NKJV)**

Paul was about to launch into the no-holds-barred truth about their sin. What he was about to say in Chapter 5 would likely be called "judging" by many. It certainly would in our culture, and even in our churches, today.

But Paul loved the Corinthian believers. They were incredibly dear to his heart. He was there when most of them professed faith in Jesus; he wanted them to grow up in their faith and, like him, live in the peace that triumphs any hard thing they would ever face.

He wanted them to discover that when their purpose was to follow Christ in all things, they would find satisfaction that far exceeded anything worldly circumstances could bring.

Paul said in another of his famous, God-given letters:

> **"Not that I am speaking of being in need, for I have learned in whatever situation I am to be content. I know how to be brought low, and I know how to abound. In any and every circumstance, I have learned the secret of facing plenty and hunger, abundance and need. I can do all things through him who strengthens me." (Phil. 4:11–13)**

And this is exactly what God wanted for those Corinthian believers—expressed through the words He inspired Paul to write. It is also what God wants for all His children—contentment, peace, and hope!

But to get there—to find that enduring peace and joy that far exceeds the bounds of this Earth— we better buckle our seat belts and get ready for some hard but always good-for-us truth. Chapter 5 is coming.

May we hold on and allow God to examine our lives with His always-good-for-us Word. Spend some time praying today, and ask the Lord to show you some of the temporary things you may be looking at for your peace. Ask the Lord to remind you of the peace you have experienced when walking with Him during hard days. Thank Him for His faithfulness.

11 *day eleven*

Please pray and read 1 Corinthians Chapter 5.

It would have been easier for Paul to just end the letter to the Corinthians right there after Chapter 4. He had clearly communicated truth. Surely they would get what he was saying, follow his example, and apply the truth to their lives.

If he just stopped there, he wouldn't risk any friendships or ruffle any feathers. No one would accuse him of being judgmental, and everyone would continue to like him.

But no

Paul was answering the higher call. Like his Savior, he was willing to sacrifice for the good of others—and sometimes that sacrifice meant speaking unpopular and hard truth. Paul knew he had to say more. He loved them too much to just hope they "caught his point." So he put his pen to the page and continued with what is now 1 Corinthians 5.

He called out their misery-making sin. He had to get uncomfortably specific about the sins of those believers in the church of Corinth. Paul held nothing back and got all in "their business." These were believers who were getting into arguments, having casual sex, and getting drunk, among other things.

Let's not miss that Paul was writing to those who had already professed the Messiah as Lord—believers.

Surely he felt the temptation to just move on to the next city, preach to the lost there, and not worry about how those Christians in Corinth were living. But for the good of the person, the good of the church, and the glory of the One True God who had saved them—and above all, because the Holy Spirit had inspired him—Paul kept writing. He kept writing because he felt that it was important to disciple the found as much as he felt the need to reach the lost. So he wrote hard words—true words.

Not to prove himself
Not to get more likes or followers
Not to "drop the mic"

He wrote hard words because he wanted them to walk in obedience. It wasn't okay to profess Jesus and then live in sin up to their eyeballs.

Friend, let's remember that though we are covered by grace because of the blood of our Savior, the pursuit of holiness is the continued call for every believer. Forsaking our flesh and following Jesus is where true joy is found this side of Heaven. It's the way of the healthy Church and the place where God, who deserves endless praise, receives the glory.

And, you know, I'm so thankful for those who loved me enough to point me to the truth and encourage me to walk away from sin when it would have been easier to say nothing at all.

Aren't you? If so, perhaps take the time today to thank someone who loved you enough to speak the truth to you. Let's encourage each other in this because, like Paul, this is how we truly love others.

12 *day twelve*

Please pray and read 1 Corinthians Chapter 5 again.

Paul began this portion of his letter to the church at Corinth (now 1 Corinthians Chapter 5 in our Bibles) by telling them that he knew about the man who was sleeping with his father's wife; they were to remove this man from the congregation.

It is important to note: we all sin. We all occasionally "step in sin," but this person was willfully, as a practice or lifestyle, "walking in it," with no plans to walk away from it.

Paul went as far as to say that they were to "deliver this man to Satan for the destruction of his flesh, so that his spirit might be saved for the day of the Lord." (1 Cor. 5:5)

It seems harsh on the surface, but the goal here was for the person caught up in sin to feel its effects (even physical ones) so that he might repent and return to obedience to the Lord and fellowship with the Church. (Also see Matt. 18:15–17.)

That was tough love.

But it was *love*.

As long as someone feels little consequence for his sin, he is not likely to flee it.

As one of my pastors used to say, "Sin is fun, at least for a while."

But if we believe God, we must remember that Romans tells us we become a slave to what we obey—"sin leading to death or obedience leading to righteousness." (Romans 6:16 NKJV)

Sin is always serious. God tells us that sin, left unchecked and allowed to "grow," leads to death. (James 1:15)

So if we truly believe God, we have to take sin very seriously and not ignore it or condone it in our own lives or the lives of our brothers—even if that means breaking fellowship so that the other person, who is caught up in unrepentant sin, might flee the sin and walk again in freedom.

When, as a body of believers, we refuse to address sin, we are being unloving to the person caught up in the sin; and the entire body is affected. Paul compared sin to leaven and how quickly it spreads. (1 Cor. 5:6–8)

Churches today that lovingly, carefully, and prayerfully confront unrepentant sin with the goal of restoration are doing the right thing both for the believer caught up in the misery-making sin and for the entire church body.

Friends, let's pray for our pastors and our leaders. Let's support them when they confront sin!

But let's also notice that this call to break fellowship is *only* toward those who call themselves believers and refuse to walk away from a lifestyle of sin. (See 1 Cor. 5:9–13.) This is an important distinction. We are not to separate ourselves from the world in our "holy huddles." We are to engage with the lost. (Note: this does not mean we engage in the sin.) It is not our place to judge them; we must pray for God-ordained conversations and love them so that they might see the Savior in us.

And let's also remember this: sometimes, we aren't the ones confronting the sin in others but are the ones who are involved in the sin ourselves.

I've been there. Have you? I've blown it. I've messed up. I've sinned. I haven't done things I should, and I've done lots of things I shouldn't. But because of the Cross, I can walk right back to Jesus and right back through the church doors to sing praises to the Lord, who forgives me over and over.

He is long-suffering and tender-hearted. He is so very faithful, even when I am not—and I'm not a lot, more than I even know! My mind cannot fathom the depths of His great love. My words can never describe the magnitude of His extraordinary kindness to me. The more I know Him, the more I love Him.

Yet I still fail Him and will fail Him more. He knew that I would fail Him over and over and over, and He still chose to die for me—and for you. No human love can ever compare. No earthly thing will ever satisfy. Yet my wayward heart will chase those empty things again and again. This is exactly why I need to be in the Word every day, reminded of truth—like His *great mercy*!

What a Savior!

All honor and glory and praise to Him!

13 *day thirteen*

Please pray and read 1 Corinthians Chapter 6.

▌ "And such were some of you . . ." (1 Cor. 6:11)

Paul just listed the kinds of sins we often glance over, considering ourselves immune from them.

You know, he was talking about the "big" sinners—the sexually immoral, idolaters, adulterers, homosexuals, thieves, greedy, drunkards, revilers, and swindlers.

No, our sins are much prettier. We often consider our sins not to be such a big deal.

We often even joke about our sins, like: "I don't repeat gossip, so you better listen closely the first time!"

Or we excuse our sins away: "I told a little white lie," or "It's just a joke . . . a dirty little joke."

Surely Paul wasn't talking to us but only to those who were caught up in the really bad stuff—the sins we don't struggle with ourselves.

And as we read this letter from this wise old apostle, we are tempted to place ourselves on Paul's side of the lectern, holding Paul's pen, and we snuggle up in our self-righteousness, ready for him to lecture those "other people."

Paul listed those "big sins." Then he said:

▌ "But you were washed, you were sanctified, you were justified in the name of the Lord Jesus Christ and by the Spirit of our God." (1 Cor. 6:11)

And then, at the end of the next verse, Paul said:

> **"But I will not be dominated by anything." (1 Cor. 6:12b)**

And then he talked about food. (1 Cor. 6:13)

Food

That doesn't seem to fit in what was about to be a discussion about fleeing sexual immorality. But it seems almost like a "pause" button . . . to caution us before we skip over this section as not "our problem." We must be very careful to remember that we—who are still flesh—are not to be dominated by *anything*.

Listen, I may not struggle with same-sex attraction, but that second piece of chocolate cake in the refrigerator is definitely calling my name. So before we consider ourselves to be immune to *any* sin struggle, let's remember we are still flesh. And because we are still flesh, we are capable of being dominated by sin.

> **"'All things are lawful for me,' but not all things are helpful." (1 Cor. 6:12)**

So before we just move on and consider ourselves to be "doing just fine," let's take a moment and ask God to examine our lives.

Is there anything "dominating us"?

Are we allowing sin to creep in our door in what we watch on TV? Are we getting good at "zinging" our spouses disrespectfully with our quick tongues? Are we spending too much time on social media?

Take a moment, and be still. Pray. Ask God. Listen for His voice.

And know this: anything He shows you is for your good and the good of those around you.

As you turn your eyes upon Him, remember that you've been washed, sanctified, and justified by the *powerful name* of the Lord Jesus Christ and the Spirit of God. He is your strength to walk away from any sin that is threatening to dominate you.

Oh, friend, let's place our eyes on Him and not excuse our own sins by simply looking at the sins of others.

God has better for us than that!

14 *day fourteen*

Please pray and reread 1 Corinthians Chapter 6:12–20.

"All things are lawful for me . . ." was a phrase the Corinthians used to justify their immoral behavior. They were living loud on the "no law, all grace" bus, and Paul was about to throw on the brakes! He didn't argue that they had indeed been set free, but he told them, "Not all things are helpful." (1 Cor. 6:12)

All things are *not helpful*, and sin will always take you further than you ever want to go . . . especially sexual sin. It is a sin against one's own body. (1 Cor. 6:18)

Paul had that same blood-bought freedom as those who would read his letter, yet he knew that what appears to be "enticing freedom" could quickly enslave and control us.

All of us

In this passage, Paul addressed the rampant sexual sin of the Corinthians with an underlying message that anything we do simply to please ourselves will yield emptiness and enslavement. In fact, the root of all sin is an attempt to please ourselves—we choose our way over God's way. But isn't it true that satisfaction from worldly things is only ever temporary and can quickly enslave us?

Paul went on to remind us all that our bodies are for the Lord:

> **"Or do you not know that your body is the temple of the Holy Spirit who is in you, whom you have from God, and you are not your own?" (1 Cor. 6:19 NKJV)**

We are not our own!

And we have a much bigger and much *better* purpose than any temporary satisfaction that could *ever* be found in food or sex or any other thing we have ever run to in our attempts to make ourselves happy.

> **"For you were bought at a price; therefore glorify God in your body and in your spirit, which are God's." (1 Cor. 6:20 NJKV)**

We who were once enemies of God have been saved by grace to glorify God with all we have! There is nothing better than that! That's where real, lasting *joy* can be found!

And grace was never meant to be a license to sin or to go back to living in such a way as to try to make ourselves happy through food or sex or the bazillion other ways we try!

As Paul Tripp says, "Joyful submission is the good life," and "If you find more joy in serving God than yourself, you know that grace has entered your door, because only grace has the power to rescue you from you."

And I need to live daily in that truth, don't you?

> **"I have been crucified with Christ; it is no longer I who live, but Christ lives in me; and the life which I now live in the flesh I live by faith in the Son of God, who loved me and gave Himself for me." (Gal. 2:20 NKJV)**

And that's the best way to live! That's the best life now!

Why not try it out for yourself in this day? Look around you, and pray for someone to serve today. Watch what happens when you do! For a hint as to what will happen, read Proverbs 11:25!

15 *day fifteen*

Please pray and read 1 Corinthians Chapter 7.

I want to preface what I am about to say with this: what I am about to say is in no way meant to excuse or explain the sinful choices of another who may have been unfaithful in marriage. Rather, this is meant as a warning to be aware of the schemes of the evil one and a call to do all we can to fortify our homes.

With that said, as I travel and speak at Christian women's events, I routinely meet single women who tell me they "long to have sex" and married women who tell me they simply "don't want to."

Doesn't that seem a little upside-down to you?

But, perhaps, it's nothing new.

Long ago, the Apostle Paul felt the need to include this in his letter to the wayward church at Corinth:

> **"Now concerning the matters about which you wrote: 'It is good for a man not to have sexual relations with a woman.' But because of the temptation to sexual immorality, each man should have his own wife and each woman her own husband. The husband should give to his wife her conjugal rights, and likewise the wife to her husband. For the wife does not have authority over her own body, but the husband does. Likewise the husband does not have authority over his own body, but the wife does. Do not deprive one another, except perhaps by agreement for a limited time, that you may devote yourselves to prayer; but then come together again, so that Satan may not tempt you because of your lack of self-control." (1 Cor. 7:1–5)**

Paul was talking about sex. And some of you thought the Bible was boring!

Things were upside-down even way back then when it came to sex. Let's not think for a moment that things aren't still upside-down or that the enemy has let his foot off the gas to destroy us with this sex thing since Paul wrote those words so long ago.

Just like way back then, we still have a "want to" problem.

We want what we can't have and don't want what we do have.

Sex outside of marriage is like a raging fire, and it will burn your house down. Don't play with it!

Paul emphatically told those believers in Corinth—and the Word is telling us also—to flee sexual immorality. (1 Cor. 6:12–20)

Flee!

Don't play with it. Don't invite it into your home. Don't visit it at the theatre. Stop watching porn. Turn off the *Game of Thrones*. Be disgusted by *Fifty Shades of Grey*. Walk away from sex outside of marriage—today.

Stop it. Stop looking for satisfaction in things that can never ever satisfy but are, in fact, hurting you and those you love.

However, to be sure, sex inside of marriage *is* a beautiful thing!

Certainly, some who are single need to pray for some "don't want to," and some who are married need to pray for some "do want to"!

Do you get my drift?

A God who is *for* you, who is for your marriage and your home and your babies, created sex—and with good reason! (And it's not just to make those babies you love with all your heart!) It's the *glue* that helps keep your marriage healthy. It actually helps protect the home you work so hard to make wonderful for those babies to live in!

And let me also tell you this, I've heard from people who have prayed for some "want to," and God has done some amazing things in their marriages.

The fact is, we can trust God when it comes to everything—including sex. He is for us. His guidance is perfect. And when we follow Him, He does "exceedingly, abundantly more than we could ask or imagine"—every single time! (Eph. 3:20)

16 *day sixteen*

Please pray and reread 1 Corinthians 7:12–40.

Yesterday, I ended with an admonition for married couples to have sex. I know some of you are dealing with hard-to-live-with spouses, and some are married to nonbelievers. For those of you who are single, widowed, or in a Christ-honoring marriage, let's simply think of this as an example of how to deal with a really hard situation.

When Paul wrote his letter to the church at Corinth, some had come to know the Lord, but their spouses had not.

Paul addressed this and encouraged those believers to consistently live out their faith so their unbelieving partner might see the Lord in their lives. (1 Cor. 7:12–16)

That's hard to do at street level, and it is an impossible calling without remembering what Paul said:

> **"You were bought at a price; do not become slaves of men." (1 Cor. 7:23 NKJV)**

No matter the hard thing we've been called to do—and living with an unbelieving spouse has to be one of the hardest—when we remember we belong to Jesus, it changes our attitude and strengthens our resolve to walk out that hard calling with an eternal perspective.

Maybe our hard calling is something other than being married to a nonbeliever. Paul talked about social status (linked to circumcision back then) and being a slave in verses 17–24. There are few slaves in our country today—in the traditional sense of the word—but maybe you are in a job where you feel treated like a slave.

The reality is that we are free because of Jesus, and that fact has some implications for how we live, even—and especially—when in a hard place. Because of Jesus, because we are His, and because we wear His Name, we are to continue to work hard and be kind, even when others aren't kind to us.

Is it easy? Nope!

But as we remember that our Lord was severely mistreated Himself, and as we recognize that our confidence is in Him even when mistreated, we are inspired to do things as He would have us because others might possibly see Jesus in us and give Him glory!

Paul also reminded those who are not slaves by the world's definition that they, as Christians, should remember they are always slaves to Christ.

We can't just live however we want because when we forget we are slaves to Christ, we fall into the trap of being slaves to men! Christians were bought with a price and are not to become slaves of men. (1 Cor. 7:24) This means we no longer operate by the world's standards or values. We've got a higher calling and a higher purpose. Paul expounded on this higher calling and higher purpose for the rest of Chapter 7.

God's Word is good. It is relevant for each day and for the real circumstances we find ourselves in. As we daily remember what Jesus did for us, it should impact how we live. And as it impacts how we live, the Gospel impacts others!

Yes, we've been bought with a price. May we glorify the One who paid it all—in this day by how we live!

Go let others see Jesus in you!

What a Savior!

17 *day seventeen*

Please pray and read 1 Corinthians Chapter 8.

As I write these words, my house is quiet. My Bible is open. I'm asking God to speak.

It's not enough that I simply learn more facts about Paul or those wayward believers at Corinth. I want those holy words of Scripture to *read me*.

I want to heed the words of James, the brother of our Lord. I don't want to be just a hearer of the Word, walking away and forgetting what God shows me about me. I want to be a doer by applying it to *my* life. (James 1:22–25)

To be honest—again, just between us—I too often read God's Word noticing how someone else needs to change when I most need to hold that mirror of God's Word up to my own nose *first* and ask God, "What are you saying to *me*, and how do you want me to apply these truths to *my* life?" I am praying, "Lord, help me, by your power, to make the changes I need to make, to love You and others better."

I don't want to miss the point of reading God's Word. It is not merely knowledge.

Paul told us, "Knowledge puffs up, but love edifies. And if anyone thinks that he knows anything, he knows nothing yet as he ought to know. But if anyone loves God, this one is known by Him." (1 Cor. 8:1b–3 NKJV)

Paul went right after the arrogance that many of the Corinthians displayed. And if we aren't careful, we may be displaying that same arrogance as well.

We want to read the Word, understand it, and apply it. But we don't want to become "puffed up" because we understand something someone else doesn't yet! Little stinks more than a prideful, arrogant Christian!

Oh, but a kind, gentle, humble heart that allows God's Word to shape how they live and love others draws others to Jesus like little else—and in doing so, they themselves are refreshed daily!

> **"For thus says the One who is high and lifted up, who inhabits eternity, whose name is Holy: 'I dwell in the high and holy place, and also with him who is of a contrite and lowly spirit, to revive the spirit of the lowly, and to revive the heart of the contrite.'" (Isa. 57:15)**

Oh, God, may Your Word daily read and refresh us! May we humbly look at ourselves before we ever look at another with it!

May we pause, pray, and ask that You continue to do the work needed in us—all for Your glory.

18 *day eighteen*

Please pray and read 1 Corinthians Chapter 8 again.

The Corinthian believers lived in a culture where idols were literally worshipped. Food and other things were offered to these false gods at ancient temples built for them.

Many Corinthian believers understood that those gods were false—that they didn't exist—so it was completely fine to eat the food that was offered to them. It seemed pretty cut and dry. (1 Cor. 8:4—6)

But some of the Corinthian believers weren't quite as mature in their understanding and had trouble eating that food with a clear conscience. They had probably lived in a culture that worshipped idols their entire lives. (Paul noted their "former association with idols" in verse 7.)

But it's curious that rather than launching into a dissertation on why the food offered to false idols was fine to eat because the gods were indeed false, Paul instead cautioned those who knew that food was fine to eat to be mindful of their weaker brother. He even called it a "sin" to wound the conscience of a weaker brother by doing something you feel free to do when they don't think it is okay.

So what do we do with this? How do we apply this to our lives?

Let's pray and ask God if there is anything in our lives that we feel free to do that might be causing a fellow believer to stumble in their conscience.

For discussion's sake—only as an example and *not* to debate drinking—let's use alcohol as an example.

Maybe you feel that drinking wine is completely fine, but you are surrounded by those who grew up in a culture that says it's absolutely wrong to drink alcohol ever. Don't insist on exercising your freedom by drinking around those people. Don't do anything that will cause your brother to stumble.

Again, alcohol is an issue that many have an opinion on and not one I want to dive into here. The point is, let's consider how our actions in any situation impact those around us.

We may be completely Scripturally right on something (those Corinthians who ate the idol food were), but let's be mindful of how we exercise and discuss those rights.

In all things, let's be careful in how we live so as not to be "puffed up" with our knowledge. (1 Cor. 8:1) We don't want to be "living so free in our freedom" that we become a stumbling block to someone else.

None of us live alone on an island. We are walking representatives of our Lord. Let's do nothing out of selfish ambition or conceit; may we carefully consider that how we live impacts those around us.

Let's remember what Paul told those in Philippi:

> **"So if there is any encouragement in Christ, any comfort from love, any participation in the Spirit, any affection and sympathy, complete my joy by being of the same mind, having the same love, being in full accord and of one mind. Do nothing from selfish ambition or conceit, but in humility count others more significant than yourselves. Let each of you look not only to his own interests, but also to the interests of others. Have this mind among yourselves, which is yours in Christ Jesus, who, though he was in the form of God, did not count equality with God a thing to be grasped, but emptied himself, by taking the form of a servant, being born in the likeness of men. And being found in human form, he humbled himself by becoming obedient to the point of death, even death on a cross. Therefore God has highly exalted him and**

bestowed on him the name that is above every name, so that at the name of Jesus every knee should bow, in heaven and on earth and under the earth, and every tongue confess that Jesus Christ is Lord, to the glory of God the Father." (Philippians 2:1–11)

May nothing we do become a stumbling block to another; we love Jesus and them!

When we are self-focused, we get sin-laden.

19 *day nineteen*

Please pray and read 1 Corinthians Chapter 9.

Paul said that though he was free, he had made himself a servant in order to win more souls to the Lord. (1 Cor. 9:19)

Paul encouraged those wayward Corinthians to remember they had a purpose that extended far beyond seeking their own happiness through sin or the freedoms they had over the law.

Paul compared the Christian life to running a race—a thing that isn't easy and takes endurance. (1 Cor. 9:24)

And then he gave them an important warning: he warned them to be careful, or they may be disqualified. (1 Cor. 9:27) He gave the example of their forefathers who had become disqualified in the wilderness. (1 Cor. 10) Those who had become disqualified in the wilderness—though fed and cared for daily in the very presence of the abiding Lord—had grumbled and complained.

And especially in our wilderness times, we often do the same.

We forget that we are cared for by the Lord, we grumble and complain, and we spin our wheels trying to fix our lives to make ourselves happy.

The children of Israel wanted more. They wanted better. They weren't living as servants on mission to bring glory to God. They were still looking for paradise on this side of Heaven—a place it can never be found. Instead of singing praises to the Lord and telling others of His deliverance, they questioned God's goodness and complained about the daily bread He provided.

The Corinthians were falling into that same trap. And we do too.

Even though we've been delivered, we still spend too much energy trying to make ourselves happy with the circumstances of *this* life.

The children of Israel and the Corinthians were self-focused and sin-laden. And those two things always seem to go hand-in-hand.

When we are self-focused, we get sin-laden.

The minute the enemy can get us consumed with ourselves and our circumstances, he gains a foothold.

But when we turn our eyes upon Jesus, gratefully thank Him for our deliverance, and purposefully, daily live to tell others of His goodness, we find that the chains of trying to create our own happiness are once again broken. We find ourselves free once more to run the race, no longer bound to this world for our joy and with eyes on the eternal.

Is it easy? Certainly not!

It's a hard race but one with an imperishable crown! (1 Cor. 9:25)

Oh, friend, let's keep running! Let's help each other keep running.

Let's remember this life is not all there is! Let's lift our eyes from this world and place them squarely on the One who works all things together for good as we follow Him! He brings beauty from ashes! He is making all things new!

What a Savior!

20 *day twenty*

Let's pause for a moment.

A few days after I wrote the ending for yesterday's devotional—"Let's remember this life is not all there is! Let's lift our eyes from this world and place them squarely on the One who works all things together for good as we follow Him! He brings beauty from ashes! He is making all things new!"—God, in His splendid goodness, gave me an amazing experience of His hand at work.

Well, let me just tell you about it.

My husband and I grabbed our bag chairs out of the back of the truck and walked toward the trail. Rain was dripping from the trees, and the night was coming. We weren't exactly sure what to expect, but we had heard about the mysterious, beautiful, synchronous fireflies in our nearby Smoky Mountains for years.

We walked a short distance and placed our chairs just off the trail facing an expansive area with large trees and low undergrowth. The stream was the only sound in the quiet woods.

But then came others—older couples, young families, groups of teens—and they all found places to sit and wait.

We were all waiting on the darkness.

As the light began to fade, we began to notice a few fireflies among the trees.

And then, as if cued by an unseen conductor, as the dark of night settled in the mountains, it happened!

Those fireflies began to all go dark together for several seconds, and then, all at once, they would light up, twinkling like thousands of Christmas lights.

It was stunning and majestic!

The synchronized pause to darkness and then the brilliant symphony of dancing lights played over and over, and it was all I could do to contain myself. I wanted to squeal at that glorious sight!

Surely God created that beautiful lightning bug dance to cause us to wonder and worship!

But maybe, just maybe, He also orchestrated that stunning act of creation to encourage us to hold on when our nights seem the darkest.

We so often find ourselves waiting in the darkest of nights in this life, but we can't forget that God is most certainly—at just the right moment—going to bring light.

And sometimes, just like with those fireflies, it takes the dark of night for our human eyes to see just how glorious and how orchestrated His light truly is.

For Christians, perhaps that is how darkness should always be viewed—as merely a prelude to the certain, glorious light that is coming.

Maybe you are sitting in the dark right now in your life. Oh, friend, hold on! He is at work! He will bring light—glorious, beautiful light!

As the Psalmist sang long ago:

> **"If I say, 'Surely the darkness shall cover me, and the light about me be night,' even the darkness is not dark to you; the night is bright as the day, for darkness is as light with you." (Psalm 139:11−12)**

Oh yes, we who know the Lord can hold on and remember:

> **"He uncovers the deep out of darkness and brings deep darkness to light."**
> **(Job 12:22)**

Always

Oh, let's go worship Him. May we be the light dancing to Him in the darkness!

21 *day twenty-one*

Please pray and read 1 Corinthians Chapter 10.

His letter was long. Page after page, Paul poured his heart out to that wayward church at Corinth.

And we stand back.

We shake our heads.

We wonder how *those* people could be so messed up when God is so good.

And then, in case we think those holy words were just for those people, Paul said:

> **"Therefore let him who thinks he stands take heed lest he fall."**
> **(1 Cor. 10:12 NKJV)**

And I know those words are meant to warn my heart.

My wayward, wandering heart
My still-flesh-filled heart that lives in a fallen world
My heart that is tempted, torn, and (honestly) flat-out tired

And I need to beware that sin is creeping at my door. Friend, none of us are immune; may Paul's words cause us all to pause.

But as we think of all that seeks to take us down, may we be encouraged by the next hope-filled, powerful words penned by that old preacher:

> **"No temptation has overtaken you that is not common to man. God is faithful, and he will not let you be tempted beyond your ability, but with the temptation he will also provide the way of escape, that you may be able to endure it."**
> **(1 Cor. 10:13)**

Those words are as true today as they were the day God had Paul write them. Our Lord is, was, and will always be our Savior! He is our very present help in our times of trouble. (Psalm 46:1) When temptation comes our way, He is always our way out!

> **"No weapon formed against you shall prosper . . ." (Isa. 54:17 NKJV)**

It will not!

As we turn our eyes upon our Rescuer—as we remember what is true about Him—we can "raise a Hallelujah in the presence of our enemies."

> *I raise a hallelujah, in the presence of my enemies*
> *I raise a hallelujah, louder than the unbelief*
> *I raise a hallelujah, my weapon is a melody*
> *I raise a hallelujah, heaven comes to fight for me.*
> (Bethel Music, "Raise a Hallelujah")

Oh, friend, may our hearts be strengthened with praise and *truth*—real truth from that Bible that may be sitting over there on your coffee table. It's your sword of truth. Pick it up! His words are so good . . . so much better than mine will ever be!

With it, you can "raise a Hallelujah" and refute the lies of the evil one!

22 *day twenty-two*

Please pray and reread 1 Corinthians Chapter 10.

Paul had just reminded the Christians caught up in sin that God is faithful and will make a way out for them when temptation comes, and then, again, he said:

> **"Therefore, my beloved, flee from idolatry." (1 Cor. 10:14)**

Flee!

He told them that God would make a way out, but they also must make an effort to walk away.

We who have been saved by the blood of Christ must stop running right back into the trouble He has saved us from! We are to flee!

If you are a believer, you can't straddle the fence. Paul was very clear when he said:

> **"You cannot drink the cup of the Lord and the cup of demons. You cannot partake of the Lord's table and the table of demons." (1 Cor. 10:21)**

Paul was pleading with the believers to understand that they were, indeed, playing with fire when they didn't flee sin. This is the kind of fire that burns down homes, destroys lives, and hurts families for generations.

He told them to flee idolatry, not because the false gods were real but because behind those idols were demonic forces of evil. (1 Cor. 10:20–21)

Dangerous
Destructive
Demonic

And friend, we can make a dangerous idol out of just about anything. Let's evaluate where we spend our time. Let's look at our priorities. We may not worship at the temple of Aphrodite or bow down to little carved images, but we all worship something daily. Paul said:

> **"Whatever you do, do all to the glory of God." (1 Cor. 10:31b)**

What's on your list for today?

It is not enough just to walk away from bad stuff; we need to get serious about doing good things to glorify the Lord.

Paul encouraged Christ-followers not to simply do things for their own advantage but to do things intentionally so that many would be saved. (1 Cor. 10:33)

The Word is telling us *all* to think about eternity—not just our own eternity but also the eternity of those around us!

Jesus really did say:

> **"Whoever is not with me is against me, and whoever does not gather with me scatters." (Matt. 12:30)**

There is no neutral with Christ! Let's carefully and prayerfully ask God to evaluate our lives.

Are we thoughtlessly participating in things with demonic roots, or are we carefully choosing the side of Christ?

God, help us flee anything not of You, and help us deliberately live lives to glorify You. May others see You in us and love You more because they know us.

"Finally, be strong in the Lord and in the strength of his might. Put on the whole armor of God, that you may be able to stand against the schemes of the devil. For we do not wrestle against flesh and blood, but against the rulers, against the authorities, against the cosmic powers over this present darkness, against the spiritual forces of evil in the heavenly places. Therefore, take up the whole armor of God, that you may be able to withstand in the evil day, and having done all, to stand firm. (Eph. 6:10–13)

Are we thoughtlessly participating in things with demonic roots, or *are we carefully choosing the side of Christ?*

23 *day twenty-three*

Please pray and read 1 Corinthians Chapter 11.

Hopefully, if you have actually met any of my kids, you are shocked to know that when they were little, they fought with each other so much that their sweet grandmother, my gracious mom, refused to keep them—except individually!

They could not get along. And that's exactly what Paul heard about that young church in Corinth. Remember, they were so bad, in fact, that word had traveled all the way to Paul in Ephesus from Corinth. That was about 354 miles and before cell phones or cars.

The Corinthian believers were famously divided. There were factions among them. (1 Cor. 11:18–19)

Paul spent the first part of this chapter giving them instructions for order, roles, and coming together as a body of believers. I can imagine him writing those words with one eyebrow raised, possibly shaking his dear old head. And then he said:

> **"Now in giving these instructions I do not praise you, since you come together not for the better but for the worse." (1 Cor. 11:17 NKJV)**

When these believers met, things were worse than if they didn't meet at all! They were famous not only for dabbling in immorality but also for the fact that they weren't getting along!

And not getting along . . . well, this might still be what some of our churches are famous for today. I once heard someone in ministry say, "Ministry would be great if it didn't involve people."

We chuckle, but if we have lived anywhere except alone on a desert island, we know it's true! People have trouble with people. Living and serving with others can be hard—challenging, frustrating, irritating, and downright discouraging! (No testimonies, please.)

We all have our favorite friends and others whom we avoid—even at church!

And we all have opinions—especially about the staff at church and how they do things.

We are quick to fire off an email about how things "should be done" and pretty slow to show up to actually help do those things.

What's more, we especially hold our pastors and their families to some ridiculously high standards.

I once spoke to a group of women that included the minister's wife. I had been encouraging those church women to have accountability partners. On break, their pastor's wife told me, "Oh, I have the whole church holding me accountable. They feel free to evaluate everything I do. If I get my hair cut, they quickly tell me what they think; their opinions are often unkind."

The truth is that we all have a tendency to look at others before we turn the mirror of God's Word on ourselves.

In giving all this instruction to the church at Corinth, God, through Paul, is also telling us to examine ourselves and evaluate our worthiness as part of the body of Christ. (1 Cor. 11:28–32)

For when we stop and look first at ourselves—before we look at others—the entire body of believers is better off.

Let's remember what Paul said back in Romans. Let's examine our own lives against these words about how to live as a Christian before we ever examine someone else:

> **"Let love be genuine. Abhor what is evil; hold fast to what is good. Love one**

another with brotherly affection. Outdo one another in showing honor. Do not be slothful in zeal, be fervent in spirit, serve the Lord. Rejoice in hope, be patient in tribulation, be constant in prayer. Contribute to the needs of the saints and seek to show hospitality. Bless those who persecute you; bless and do not curse them. Rejoice with those who rejoice, weep with those who weep. Live in harmony with one another. Do not be haughty, but associate with the lowly. Never be wise in your own sight. Repay no one evil for evil, but give thought to do what is honorable in the sight of all. If possible, so far as it depends on you, live peaceably with all." (Romans 12:9–18)

Because when we live this way, we are better, the Church is better, and those who aren't yet a part of the Church might want to join us too!

And your grandma might want to hang out with you when you are all together!

24 *day twenty-four*

Please pray and read 1 Corinthians Chapter 12.

Has Scripture ever just come alive when you least expected it? For me, it was 1 Corinthians 12 in a public restroom at the hospital.

In that passage, Paul famously talked about spiritual gifts and the Church being one body with many members. He said:

> **"But as it is, God arranged the members in the body, each one of them, as he chose." (1 Cor. 12:18)**

He talked about how each part is important, and he said that the parts that "seem to be weaker are indispensable." (1 Cor. 12:18, 22)

Each one of us has an indispensable role in the body of Christ. No matter where life has us, we have a calling on our lives as believers.

Let me tell you more about that day and the person I met in the hospital's public restroom.

Her presence filled the room like royalty. She held the mop like a queen's scepter as she prepared to clean the hospital restroom. I immediately noticed her dazzling smile as our eyes met, and something in me told me she was a daughter of the King.

For the next several moments, this beautiful woman and I talked. She asked me why I found myself at the hospital, and I explained about my mom's health scare. She told me how hard she worked to keep germs at bay for the patients, and she assured me that she knew we had some great nurses where we were.

As mothers often do, we shared about our kids, and the Jesus-in-us connected in just a few moments. She told me she would pray for my family. My heart was lifted. She encouraged my soul—right there in the ladies' restroom.

I thought about how this precious woman was beautifully fulfilling her calling and how she was used by God to minister to me in that moment.

And I thought of Mary's song of praise—the words that rolled off Mary's tongue after embracing the also-pregnant Elizabeth.

The soul of this beautiful janitor in the hospital bathroom magnified the Lord like Mary's:

> **"And Mary said, 'My soul magnifies the Lord, and my spirit rejoices in God my Savior, for he has looked on the humble estate of his servant. For behold, from now on all generations will call me blessed; for he who is mighty has done great things for me, and holy is his name. And his mercy is for those who fear him from generation to generation. He has shown strength with his arm; he has scattered the proud in the thoughts of their hearts; he has brought down the mighty from their thrones and exalted those of humble estate . . .'" (Luke 1:46–52)**

Friend, no matter where we find ourselves, no matter what our position, we each have an opportunity to magnify the Lord.

Oftentimes, we think only preachers and speakers and those on stage are the ones with high callings. But that doesn't seem to fit with the way God has often worked in Scripture and how I see Him work today. God has always been in the business of doing mighty things with willing, humble hearts. (1 Cor. 1:26–31)

And I can find no place in Scripture that leads me to believe that the reward in Heaven for the mega-church pastor will be any more than that of the beautiful janitor who does her job well.

God is certainly not impressed by position and power like our human hearts tend to be.

Instead, He works so often in unexpected places and through ordinary people to do amazing things. Think about it: if God chose a poor teenage girl to bring His Son into the world, don't think for a moment that He doesn't want to use you right where you are, where you work, where you shop, and on the street where you live.

You don't need a title when you've got a calling! And friend, you've got a calling!

We who know Jesus as Lord—we who are sons and daughters of the King—need to hold our heads high, embrace the calling on our lives, and point others to the Savior!

This is true even—and especially—when the place God has called us to may be hard.

Many of us are called to the hard places . . . or we will be one day.

There are those who endure the hard marriages, those who care for the elderly parent, and those who patiently raise the child with special needs who will never leave home. There are those who love the prodigals, those who serve the homeless, and those who pick up the broken and addicted. There are those who study the Word and teach in the small churches, those who care for the orphans and seek out the lonely, and those who love the hard-to-love.

There is no trophy for the ones who lay down their lives for others day in and day out. They are rarely thanked and often go unnoticed by a world that celebrates self, selfies, and social media followers.

But make no mistake. They are warriors. The beautiful janitor in the bathroom, those who care for the sick and the broken, those who love the unlovely, and those who get up day after day to serve in the hard ministries—they are all stealth soldiers in a Kingdom that is powerfully advancing!

And they daily die to themselves—their desires and their needs. But it is there that they find they truly live. These suffering soldier saints don't just cognitively believe in the crucifixion; they have, themselves, been crucified with Christ. They've been set free from the bondage of the emptiness of temporary worldly satisfaction. They've answered a higher calling to a better, eternal purpose.

Yes, they've been hurt, knocked down, scarred, and disappointed in the battle. But their eyes remain steadily on the eternal, better prize. And through them, God is bringing amazing light into the darkest corners of darkness and setting captives free.

As I have talked to these people over the years, they all tell me their strength is not their own. Mere human love would have walked away long ago. On their own, they would have stopped caring, but Jesus is the source of their strength and their love.

Daily, they run to and place their hope in the One True King, who they know will right all the wrongs, heal all the wounds, and make all things new. And as they quietly suffer and patiently serve, a lost world sees Jesus in them. Dying people catch a glimpse in them of what it means to truly live.

And these warriors—these disciples—keep making more disciples, and the Kingdom of God advances . . . one person, one decision, and one day at a time.

Oh, friend, oh, soldier, be encouraged! Encourage others to keep on keeping on! God is at work in you and through you. He sees you. And one day, our eyes will behold His glory, and our faith will become sight. Rejoice; victory belongs to our Lord!

25 *day twenty-five*

Please pray and read 1 Corinthians Chapter 13.

It seems a bit strange that a man who had caused such tremendous suffering to others before coming to Christ—and then suffered so incredibly much himself, even being stoned until his persecutors thought he was dead—wrote what are, perhaps, the most famous words about love ever written.

We quote 1 Corinthians 13 at weddings. This passage has been repeatedly preached in most of our churches, and many of us have it framed in our homes.

Love

We all love *love*.

But we need to pay attention to the placement of Paul's words on love.

Remember, we are reading a letter.

That church at Corinth would have sat together reading Paul's words aloud. They would not have paused at chapters; those delineations were added later to our Bibles (around 1551) to help us identify passages.

Those who heard about love would have just heard Paul talk about spiritual gifts in his letter.

Remember, Paul was concerned that those young believers were fighting over which spiritual gifts were best and getting "puffed up" over having certain gifts. (1 Cor. 12)

But Paul said, in effect, that you can have any spiritual gift there is, even using it to "remove mountains," but if you use your gift without love, "it profits nothing." (1 Cor. 13:1–3)

Nothing

Paul even compared this unloving use of gifts to pagan worship. (1 Cor. 13:1) The pagans used the banging of brass and cymbals to worship false gods.

Paul said that the things we attempt to do for God, without love, are worthless and not of God.

It's like worship to a false god.

With this in mind, Paul then defined real love.

So let's take a moment and, once again, prayerfully ask God to hold the mirror of His precious Word up to our lives when it comes to how we love others:

> **"Love is patient and kind; love does not envy or boast; it is not arrogant or rude. It does not insist on its own way; it is not irritable or resentful; it does not rejoice at wrongdoing but rejoices with the truth. Love bears all things, believes all things, hopes all things, endures all things." (1 Cor. 13:4–7)**

That's some good, hard stuff.

Paul told those Corinthians to understand what love truly is and evaluate their actions with it—and he is telling us that too.

He said it was time to put away childish things and grow up. (1 Cor. 13:11)

And if you are hanging in here reading this, I'm guessing you, like me, want God to help you keep "growing up" in Him.

If we sincerely want to grow in the Lord, if we genuinely want what we do to have any Kingdom impact at all, and if we truly want our works to be more than a worthless clanging cymbal, we have to grow in love.

But how do we do this?

We run to the Source of love—our Lord. We ask Him to fill us up to overflow into the lives of others.

As He always is, He will be our strength to do what we could never do on our own. As we focus on His love for us, and as we love Him, we can freely and supernaturally love others—beyond ourselves. And as we do that, we will be more like our Savior.

When asked what the greatest commandment was, our Lord replied:

> **"You shall love the Lord your God with all your heart and with all your soul and with all your mind. This is the great and first commandment. And a second is like it: You shall love your neighbor as yourself." (Matt. 22:37–39)**

Spend some time in prayer today. Ask the Lord to show you how you can love others more.

26 *day twenty-six*

Please pray and reread 1 Corinthians 13:12.

I sat trying to restrain myself from the bowl of chips and salsa when it happened.

She poked my arm and looked up at me, proclaiming, "*This* is a picture of God." She was only four then, and she proudly held up her crayon drawing—a large, squiggly circle surrounding two odd-shaped, bulging eyes.

Speechless for a moment, I thought about the holiness of the Most High God, sitting on the eternal throne, and the fact that no one has ever seen Him. I knew the ancient Jews reverently hesitated to even write His name.

Yet there my little niece sat, smiling from ear to ear, and I believe God must have been smiling too. "Oh, Ann Claire, I know God must be so happy that you were thinking enough about Him to draw a picture of Him. I bet you made Him smile," I said. She seemed satisfied with my response, but I have thought about her picture for years. I thought about it again as I read Paul's words in 1 Corinthians 13:12 where he described the way we see God now as "dimly," but one day, it will be "face to face."

I think we all draw pictures of God, though some have given Him so little thought that their pictures are quite featureless. Others base their pictures on the few words they heard about Him long ago in a Sunday school class or vacation Bible school. And some draw their pictures from completely false information. For many, their pictures are just copies of what others have told them their pictures should look like.

But what about you? What does *your* picture of God look like?

No one has seen Him, yet God desires to reveal Himself to us. Honestly, how much thought have you given the God of the Universe—your Creator and the One who holds eternity in His hands?

Do you desire to intimately know Him? Do you search the Scriptures for the minutest details of His character?

Is He smiling in your picture? Are His arms wide open? Is He far removed from you, or are you walking arm in arm, talking about everything as He would want? Do His eyes twinkle with a sense of humor, as when He called Samuel? (1 Sam. 3)

Is He strong, even fearsome, but still approachable? Is He completely loving and all good yet simultaneously the Righteous Judge?

Does He hold you close, even when you don't understand Him? I think about how Gideon asked:

> **"If the LORD is with us, why has all this happened to us?" (Judges 6:13)**

Is your picture black and white or full of color and endless, unfathomable detail?

Is He your friend who sticks closer than a brother? (Prov. 18:24)

Even though you have not seen Him, may you exclaim with your heart as Job did:

> **"My ears had heard of you, but now my eyes have seen you." (Job 42:5 NIV)**

Oh, friend, what does your picture of God really look like? Is it based on truth from His Word and revelation of the Holy Spirit, or do you rely only on what you occasionally hear, along with faint recollections from long ago? Do you daily seek to add to your painting accurately? Do you delight in His revelations of Himself?

Do praise songs flood your heart with images you have painted of Him? Oh, He is indescribable, and our artwork will never be complete!

The Apostle Paul told the Corinthians:

> **"For now we see in a mirror dimly, but then face to face. Now I know in part; then I shall know fully, even as I have been fully known." (1 Cor. 13:12)**

Oh, can you imagine? One day we will see God face to face!

You are beautiful beyond description
Too marvelous for words
Too wonderful for comprehension
Like nothing ever seen or heard
Who can grasp your infinite mercy?
Who can fathom the depth of your love?
You are beautiful beyond description
Majesty, enthroned above
(Sovereign Grace Music, "I Stand in Awe")

Oh, Father, may our hearts never grow cold. May we desire to know You better daily. May we pursue *You* through Your Word. Help us to rise above the distractions of this life, and help us to see You in this day. Open our eyes to Your infinite goodness. Help us to praise You more. Oh, God, I know my picture of You can never contain your marvelous majesty—yet I want to see You. You are God with us—Most High, Amazing God with me! Let me say in this life, "My ears had heard of You, but now my eyes see You!"

It is so often in those "away-from-the-spotlight" moments that *others will be encouraged to hold on, to see Jesus, and to grow in their faith.*

27 *day twenty-seven*

Please pray and read 1 Corinthians Chapter 14.

You know, we can make a mess out of anything when we make it about us.

Our human hearts love attention. They always have. We love the stage and the applause. We love to know more than others around us and be known. I am amazed at the multitude of people who post videos about anything and everything, vying for likes and shares. So many want to be famous.

Even hearts that have found Jesus can be deceived into looking for satisfaction in fleeting things, like the praise of others.

And the Corinthians were no different. (1 Cor. 14)

Paul had been talking to them about using their spiritual gifts to love others. (1 Cor. 13; see Day 24.)

But they desired what they considered the "big gifts"—the gifts that would draw a crowd (like speaking in tongues) rather than those that would encourage and strengthen the body. (1 Cor. 14:4)

Ministry, just like anything else, can be seductive.

And those of us who seek to serve the Lord need to continually check our hearts and make sure we aren't seeking the praise of others more than the praise of God.

So often, the greatest Kingdom impact comes not from the "big things" we think we are doing but often in the "smaller ways" that don't seem like big things at the time—things like soft words over a cup of coffee with a hurting friend.

It is often when we "love small" that we minister the biggest—the quiet prayers, the card, the phone call, the silent deed, the times we truly get over ourselves enough to love others with no desire or even opportunity for recognition!

It is so often in those "away-from-the-spotlight" moments that others will be encouraged to hold on, to see Jesus, and to grow in their faith.

As we daily love others, without regard to being known, Jesus is made known.

The Gospel spreads.

The Kingdom advances.

Yes, when we love "small," seeking to serve the Lord wherever He has us, we minister big!

Glory to Jesus!

Spend a few moments in prayer. Ask the Lord to help you see how you might love someone else with no chance of glory for yourself. Perhaps consider doing something anonymously. Ask the Lord to help you see others as He does and run to those in need, even when no one else sees you . . . except the Lord, who delights in that kind of service.

28 *day twenty-eight*

Please pray and reread 1 Corinthians 14:26–40.

I was tempted to skip past part of this passage. Of course, Paul's discussion regarding order in the church is straightforward, and we all agree that order is a good thing.

But speaking in tongues and the role of women in the church can cause some controversy.

So have a good day. Talk to you later.

Seriously, however tempted I might be to skip over passages that seem confusing or controversial, I simply cannot, and neither should you.

Let's slow down. Let's chew on it. Let's ask God to help us understand what He is saying, and let's endeavor to follow Him closer, even if that means digging deeper to do so.

First, God's Word is perfect. It is Holy Spirit inspired. But our interpretation is not always perfect, so we want to be very careful and prayerful in how we read and apply the Word.

In this passage, it seems that Paul was working to clarify some confusion—in this case, regarding tongues. (See 1 Cor. 14:26–33.) He said the motive for speaking in tongues should be for edification; there should be order, and there should be an interpreter. Otherwise, the person should "speak to himself and to God." (1 Cor. 14:28)

But then we come to verses 34–35 about women not speaking in the church. And I feel confused. However, I literally just read:

> **"God is not the author of confusion but of peace, as in all the churches of the saints." (1 Cor. 14:33 NKJV)**

Now, remember, we want to always read the Word with the Word. So when a passage seems confusing on the surface, we should look to see if the subject is addressed in other places. I like to pull out commentaries to help me with this.

As I study the passage about women not speaking in church, I realize Paul had previously discussed women praying and prophesying back in 1 Cor. 11:5, so he could not be completely forbidding women from speaking in church.

If we look just before verses 34 and 35, we see Paul had been discussing *judging* and *interpreting* prophecy and tongues. Most commentators believe that Paul was saying that women can pray and prophesy, but they are not to take the *authority* to judge prophecies or interpret tongues.

The issue, then, is not that women are not to speak or even serve in the church; the issue is with what authority they may take. This interpretation is consistent with God's Word in 1 Timothy 2:12 when it comes to the role of women. Women are not to take authority over men in the church setting. This has to do with order. We know women like Miriam, Deborah, and Priscilla were used by God and even taught others, but they did not take authority over men in their teaching within the church setting.

Most of the time, when I have a question about the Word, I find the Lord will use the Holy Spirit to help me come to an understanding as I prayerfully look to other parts of the Bible for clarification. The Word clarifies the Word. Let's remember this.

This is part of testing everything and holding on to the good. And we want to test everything we hear and read. We want to follow the Lord as closely as possible and obey Him with all our hearts. Surely we can always trust Him more than we trust ourselves. We can know that His Word—even when it may go against the culture or what might *feel* right to us—is always for our good because God is for our good. We can trust Him more than we can trust ourselves.

29 *day twenty-nine*

Please pray and read 1 Corinthians Chapter 15.

How much would you give so someone else might live?

Let me tell you what caused me to think about this: some folks who are dear to me are facing an unjust judgment. Because of another's dishonesty, they are facing a penalty of a large amount of money. It's more than they have.

One of them recently said, "If somehow they could see Jesus in us and come to know Him, I'd gladly pay that much. It would be worth it."

Gulp
Talk about convicting

I asked myself, how much would I be willing to spend for another to come to know the Lord?

What about you? $100,000? $50,000? $5,000?

What about for someone who has hurt you or wants to hurt you?

How much would be too much to give for that really-not-nice lost person if it meant they would be saved from Hell?

We all say we want others to come to know Jesus but at what cost to ourselves?

How much *time* would we give?

What *inconvenience* or *insult* would we endure?

Just how *long* of a hard road might we be willing to walk in order for another to see Jesus in us?

And the thing is, when we put it in terms of writing a check, we need to remember this: Jesus paid a debt for us that we could never pay!

In order to love others and endure hard things for the cause of Christ, we shouldn't see ourselves in the position of the one writing the check but in the grateful position of the one for whom the check has already been written!

We have to continually focus on that!

And as Paul began to close his first letter to those Corinthians, he reminded them to remember the Gospel—to keep the first thing first. (1 Cor. 15:1–3)

While we were His enemies, Jesus paid it all so we might live! God gave it all—His greatest treasure for us!

If we remember the Gospel, if our eyes are on the prize that is Christ Jesus, and if we are disciples who desire to make disciples, then every situation we face should be viewed as an opportunity for someone else to see Jesus in us.

May God use all we are, all we have, and every trial we face for His glory!

And when hard things come—when we are asked to give more than we feel we can—it is usually for reasons much bigger than our human eyes can see.

Oh, glory to Him!

Praise the One who paid my debt!

"For I delivered to you as of first importance what I also received: that Christ died for our sins in accordance with the Scriptures . . ." (1 Cor. 15:3)

Ask the Lord to show you anything you are withholding from His Kingdom purposes. Ask Him to help you trust Him to lay everything at His feet for His glory and the good of others—and yourself.

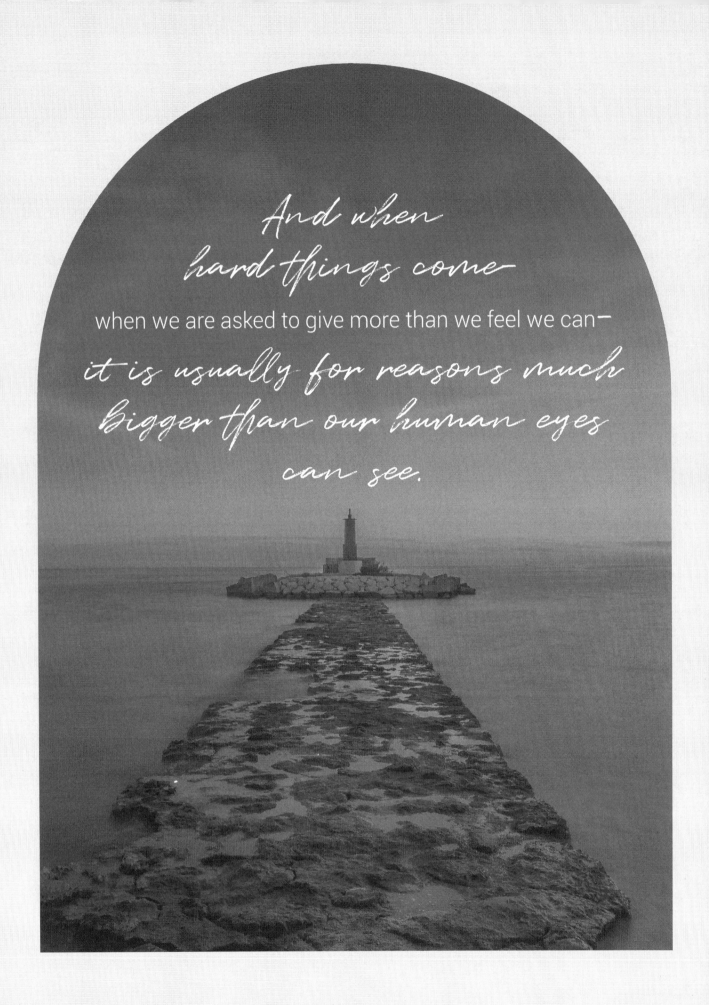

And when
hard things come
when we are asked to give more than we feel we can—
it is usually for reasons much
bigger than our human eyes
can see.

30 *day thirty*

Please pray and reread 1 Corinthians Chapter 15.

Paul had once persecuted the Church. (1 Cor. 15:9) We can't just skip lightly over the ugly weight of those words.

Did drops of Stephen's blood splash on his sandals? Did Paul remember the screams as he had men and women of The Way dragged from their homes and imprisoned? Were the tears of their children still on his mind? Did he think about the votes he had cast for their floggings and even for their deaths?

Oh, Paul remembered his horrible sins.

I remember mine, and I am sure you remember yours as well.

But those who know the Savior have also tasted grace—glorious rivers of grace bought when the Perfect Lamb defeated death and rose to life!

Paul's pen was about to form the famous, true words:

> **"'O Death, where is your sting? O Hades, where is your victory?' The sting of death is sin, and the strength of sin is the law. But thanks be to God, who gives us the victory through our Lord Jesus Christ." (1 Cor. 15:55–57 NKJV)**

But before he could get to those famous words, he had to set their thinking straight—perhaps some of ours too.

Some of the Corinthians were arguing that there was no resurrection of the dead, so Paul told them that without the resurrection, they would still be in their sins. (1 Cor. 15:17)

But because Jesus defeated death, we who have called on His Name are no longer "in our sins." Can you imagine how much this meant to Paul (formerly Saul, who had persecuted the Church)?

This should also mean so very much to us! No matter what we have done, no matter what came to your mind just then, we who believe have been washed clean!

Forever clean

We have been set free from the penalty we deserve for the ugly sins we remember.

Some of you need to read that last sentence again!

Hallelujah! Praise the Lord!

And Paul, knowing full well what he had done, also remembered what Jesus did and said:

> **"But by the grace of God I am what I am, and his grace toward me was not in vain. On the contrary, I worked harder than any of them, though it was not I, but the grace of God that is with me." (1 Cor. 15:10)**

Paul knew he had been forgiven much and spent the rest of his life boldly and confidently living for Christ—not walking around in shame—and spreading the good news of the Gospel wherever his sandaled feet took him!

Like the parable Jesus told in Luke 7:36–50, those who know they have had great debt forgiven love much. (Oh, go read it. It is so good!)

So as the evil one reminds us today of our past sins, we have a choice to make.

Shall we choose to be bound by the shame, as the enemy certainly would hope?

Or shall we, with grateful hearts, be amazed at the grace of God once more and be even more determined to give all we have to obey and serve our Lord, the One who paid all our debt?

Yes, I know my sins are many. The enemy has reminded me often.

But God
But grace

Because He lives—because I serve a *risen Savior*—I can face tomorrow and serve my precious King with all I have! (1 Cor. 15:20)

What about you?

Glory to Him!

Spend some time today thanking the Lord for His mercy and grace toward you.

*No one but God
can ever be enough for you.*

You aren't enough for yourself.

You were never meant to be enough.

31 *day thirty-one*

Please pray and reread 1 Corinthians 15:28.

I hear it so much: "You are enough."

I read Scripture, and I know it is a lie.

We are not ever—nor were we intended to be, nor could we ever be—*enough*.

We were always meant to be dependent on our Savior.

Paul wrote in his letter to the church in Rome that in God, never in ourselves, is life and peace. (Rom 8:6)

The mind set on the flesh is death and enmity against God and can never please God. (Rom. 8:5–8)

Paul told the church at Corinth that one day, God would put every power under His feet and restore things to their proper order.

The end of 1 Cor. 15:28 says all this will happen so "that God may be all in all."

But until then, we seem to be stuck on trying to make every other thing and person—except God—our "all in all," including ourselves.

No one but God can ever be enough for you. You aren't enough for yourself. You were never meant to be enough.

It is easy to get pumped up from the popular motivational posts and speeches of our day touting "you are enough," but that will only carry us about five minutes before we become frustrated in trying to be "enough."

If we are honest, we know, "We don't have this!"

Only Jesus

In glorious dependency on *Him* are life and peace.

When we run on our own strength and look for our "enough" in ourselves, we come up woefully short.

But as we turn our eyes on Jesus, we find help, strength, hope, and peace far greater than anything we will ever find by looking inward.

I love this song by Jeremy Camp. It helps me remember I don't have to be enough—because Jesus is!

> *In this obsession with the things this world says make us happy*
> *Can't see the slaves we are in all the searching all the grasping*
> *Like we deserve much more than all these blessing we're holding*
> *So now I'm running free into an ocean of mercy unending*
>
> *So come and empty me*
> *So that it's you I breathe*
> *I want my life to be*
> *Only Christ in me*
> *So I will fix my eyes*
> *'Cause you're my source of life*
> *I need the world to see*

That it's Christ in me
That it's Christ in me

Done with what holds me down the things I once was chasing after
Throw off these heavy chains that I have let become my master
So now I'm running free into an ocean of mercy unending

So come and empty me
So that it's you I breathe
I want my life to be
Only Christ in me
So I will fix my eyes
'Cause you're my source of life
I need the world to see
That it's Christ in me
That it's Christ in me
(Jeremy Camp, "Christ in Me")

What a Savior!

32 *day thirty-two*

Please pray and reread 1 Corinthians 15:30–35.

If Christians are wrong, if the dead aren't raised, then "let us eat and drink, for tomorrow we die." (1 Cor. 15:32)

But if we truly believe what we say we believe—that Jesus conquered death and this life is far from all there is—then we better pay attention to how we live.

Today
This day

And a big determining factor of how well we live is who we hang around.

> **"Don't be deceived. 'Evil company corrupts good habits.'" (1 Cor. 15:33 NKJV)**

It did long ago when Paul wrote those words. It always has. It always will.

Paul was dealing with people who literally denied the resurrection and others who carelessly lived their lives as if they believed this life is all there is.

Once again, Paul held nothing back.

He didn't mince words. He didn't "beat around the bush," as my grandpa used to say.

Paul loved those Corinthians enough to want them to walk in truth. (I wonder, do we love others like this?)

With every word inspired by God, Paul pleaded with them to wake up and understand the dire consequences that come from believing this life is all that matters and living with little regard for the souls of others.

He wrote that he so believed what he was saying that he was daily willing to die for it. (1 Cor. 15:31–32) He told them:

> **"Wake up from your drunken stupor . . ." (1 Cor. 15:34)**

Whether we are drunk on alcohol or just drunk on ourselves, it's to our shame if people around us can't see any hint of Jesus in us.

Shame

Paul called it what it was then and what it still is today.

It's a shame that something as significant as salvation through faith in Jesus could happen to you, and you live your life as if it never even happened!

But that's exactly how some in that church at Corinth were living and how some of us live today.

Friend, does anyone know you love Jesus?

Do they see Him in you?

Do you live to follow Him and tell others about Him?

Is grace still *amazing* to you?

Oh, friend, maybe you just need to stop and remember. Maybe your heart needs to worship once again. Perhaps you need to think back to your rescue and praise the Savior that His mercies are still new every morning.

Yesterday is gone. Maybe you've been living like there is no eternal tomorrow.

But today, oh, today is a new day to live so others might see Him in you!

And eternity with Him . . . that's a real thing and better than anything our hearts could ever hold in this life!

What a Savior!

And here's a challenge: if you think there is any possibility that those you love might not know you love Jesus, will you tell them? Maybe write it down. Perhaps send a letter, an email, or even a text, and let others know about the time you came to know the Lord.

It isn't easy.
It's far from easy.

*But as we daily,
over and over,
surrender our expectations
for how things should go—*
as we lay down our need to always understand
and explain what God is doing—and, instead,
simply follow Him in faith,

*we will reap a bountiful
harvest of peace.*

33 *day thirty-three*

Please pray and reread 1 Corinthians 15:35–37.

There will always be things about God that we don't understand—things we can't explain.

Right now, in my life and in the lives of those I know and love, there are hard things happening that just don't make sense to me.

I can't tell you just how God is bringing beauty from some of the ashes I see—not yet, anyway.

And as we come to 1 Corinthians 15:35–37, Paul was trying to help the Corinthians understand that God does what He pleases and that we don't have to understand or explain Him to keep believing Him.

Some of the Corinthians were stuck because they couldn't understand how God could possibly raise the dead.

Some of us get stuck, too, when it seems impossible for God to bring something good from the hard, sad things we see.

If we are honest, we all sometimes expect God to do things just like we want and in ways we can readily explain.

We often treat Him like our vending machine. We send up a prayer and give Him what we consider a reasonable time to answer in a way we would choose.

When we don't understand or like the answer, we often get stuck. "How could God let *that* happen?" we think.

Why would I lose that baby? Why would she get cancer? Why would he leave me? Why would I have those parents? Why would my business fail? Why would . . .

In our questioning—in those moments where we just can't see how God could possibly bring something good from something we don't understand—some of us are tempted to walk away.

But do we have to be able to explain God in order to follow Him and trust Him?

And would you really find a god who does everything just as you would expect to be God at all?

As a seed is buried in the ground and miraculously becomes a fruit-bearing plant, we must learn to bury our expectations for how and when God should act and, instead, trust Him to bring fruit in His time. (1 Cor. 15:37–38)

It isn't easy. It's far from easy. But as we daily, over and over, surrender our expectations for how things should go—as we lay down our need to always understand and explain what God is doing—and, instead, simply follow Him in faith, we will reap a bountiful harvest of peace.

God alone is good. He sees things we can't. He is all-powerful. He does the impossible. He brings beauty from ashes.

> **"And we know that for those who love God all things work together for good, for those who are called according to his purpose." (Rom. 8:28)**

Oh, friend, let's keep loving and trusting God even when we don't understand. Let's encourage each other. Let's rest in the fact that He is God—and we are not. Let's take one day at a time and trust Him to use even the hardest things in our lives for our good and His glory. Spend some time today asking the Lord to help you give Him the things you may not understand. Ask Him to help you trust Him more and walk in peace. He can. He will . . . one day at a time.

34 *day thirty-four*

Please pray and reread 1 Corinthians 15:35–58.

I knew these powerful words were coming toward the end of Paul's letter. I've been ready for them. I'm *so* ready for them:

> **"Death is swallowed up in victory. O Death, where is your sting? O Hades, where is your victory?" (1 Cor. 15:54–55 NKJV)**

I've held on to those hope-giving, true words through tears over and over in my life.

Like most of you, I've felt the sting of death.

Too close
Too personal
Too many times

My heart still aches when I think of Rick. If you've read my story, you know the tragedy surrounding my first husband's death. (My book *Truth to Hold On To* is available on Amazon.)

And when I think of the deep sting of death, I also think of my friend's baby.

Like my son, he was born way too early. For nearly eight months, he fought to live, but he never went home from the hospital.

The day he died, a nurse called me to tell me my friend wanted to do one last thing for her son. She wanted to give him a bath before the funeral home came to get his little body, and she wanted me to help.

I cried buckets of tears as I drove to the hospital. I begged God to hold me together so I could hold that little baby while she washed him.

The memory of his tiny, lifeless body in my arms as his broken-hearted momma did one last thing for him will always remind me of the deep, painful sting of death.

And death always feels wrong.

Always

Even when the old leave us, our hearts still ache, and our tears still pour like rain.

I still miss my papaw's laugh. I adored him and his way of saying things. I will never forget the time he told me, "Kim, when most people get mad, they need to count to ten. You have enough temper that you need to count to 100." And then he'd laugh and hug me—what I'd give for one of his hugs right now.

Yes, we all know the sting of death far too well.

But those who know Jesus know this life is not all there is!

Thanks be to God! There is a glorious resurrection for those in Christ!

> "I tell you this, brothers: flesh and blood cannot inherit the kingdom of God, nor does the perishable inherit the imperishable. Behold! I tell you a mystery. We shall not all sleep, but we shall all be changed, in a moment, in the twinkling of an eye, at the last trumpet. For the trumpet will sound, and the dead will be raised imperishable, and we shall be changed. For this perishable body must put on the imperishable, and this mortal body must put on immortality. When the perishable puts on the imperishable, and the mortal puts on immortality, then shall come to pass the saying that is written:
> 'Death is swallowed up in victory.'

> 'O death, where is your victory?
> O death, where is your sting?'"
> (1 Cor. 15:50–55)

One day
One glorious day

Thanks be to God that there is eternal victory over death through Jesus Christ! (1 Cor. 15:57)

What hope
What truth to hold on to

And because of this truth, we who mourn can mourn with hope—real hope!

> "Then I saw a new heaven and a new earth, for the first heaven and the first earth had passed away, and the sea was no more. And I saw the holy city, new Jerusalem, coming down out of heaven from God, prepared as a bride adorned for her husband. And I heard a loud voice from the throne saying, 'Behold, the dwelling place of God is with man. He will dwell with them, and they will be his people, and God himself will be with them as their God. He will wipe away every tear from their eyes, and death shall be no more, neither shall there be mourning, nor crying, nor pain anymore, for the former things have passed away.' And he who was seated on the throne said, 'Behold, I am making all things new.' Also he said, 'Write this down, for these words are trustworthy and true.'" (Rev. 21:1–5)

These words are trustworthy and true! Oh, friend, read the Word! Hold on to the Word! Walk forward in truth!

And let's be people who live to tell others of the One who defeated death so we might live!

"O death, where is your sting?"

35 *day thirty-five*

Please pray and read 1 Corinthians 15:58 and 1 Corinthians Chapter 16.

Paul was about to close one of the most famous letters ever written.

He had poured out his heart. His words were breathed by the Most High to equip us for what we've been called to do.

They are truth to hold on to, hope to be had, and joy to be found when we allow them to sink deep inside our hearts.

They are instructions for how we are to live this very day.

Paul told all those who wear the Name of Christ—and he is telling you and me:

> **"Therefore, my beloved brethren, be steadfast, immovable, always abounding in the work of the Lord, knowing that your labor is not in vain in the Lord."**
> **(1 Cor. 15:58 NKJV)**

We aren't serving the Lord for nothing. There is a purpose far greater than anything our human eyes can see! Paul then said:

> **"Watch, stand fast in the faith, be brave, be strong. Let all that you do be done with love." (1 Cor. 16:13–14 NKJV)**

God has given us very clear instructions through Paul's pen about how to live out our faith.

Stand fast. Be brave. Be strong. Do everything with love.

There are a whole lot of verbs in these words at the end of this letter! And as James wrote, we can't just be hearers of the Word; we are to be doers! (James 1:22)

If we want the blessing, we have to live the Word and not just read it!

We are to apply it to our lives in the things that come at us each day.

And these holy words that we are to live by are called "daily bread," for we can no more store them up from a once-a-week-glance on Sunday than the Israelites could store up manna in the desert. (Deut. 8:3)

We need God's Word every single day! We need to read it and re-read it.

Our weak flesh needs to be reminded of the truth. We need to be encouraged daily. We need truth to hold on to every second! We need to know He is the lifter of our heads for everything we will ever face. We must rest in His unending goodness. We need to remember He is strength and power far beyond anything we can muster on our own. We must stand on the fact that He will never leave us or forsake us.

God tells us all these things and so much more in this letter and throughout His Word.

Friend, you really don't need my words; you've got His!

But because our flesh is weak, we all get weary and forget, and we have an enemy who has come only to rob, kill, and destroy, we desperately need to encourage one another with truth from the Word. I hope you have found encouragement in this devotional so far.

And as we keep seeking God through His Word, the Holy Spirit will help us follow our Lord through the good days and the hard ones.

As we walk with Him—steadfast, immovable, abounding in the work of the Lord—our labor won't be in vain! (1 Cor. 15:58)

The Kingdom will advance!

Friends, let's be intentional to encourage each other to watch, stand fast in the faith, be brave, and be strong. Let all that we do be done with love. (1 Cor. 16:13–14)

Oh, how I love these words in Paul's first letter to the church at Corinth. Thank you for studying 1 Corinthians with me! It's been good for my heart. May we run to God's Word daily, for there is no substitute for what it will do in and through us!

Are you ready for the second letter to the church at Corinth?

What a Savior!

second corinthians

INTRODUCTION

As I pick up Paul's second letter to the church at Corinth, I am reminded of just how much I need God and His Word.

Over and over in Scripture—and also over and over in my life and the lives of others I observe—I am reminded that we *absolutely* can't do things in our own strength.

We can't. We weren't made to do so.

We were made for joyful dependence on the Rock who is Christ the Lord.

Yes, we need Him for salvation and eternity; but we also need Him for the struggles of this very day on this side of Heaven. We need His counsel. We need His wisdom. We need His *power* and His *abiding presence*.

We need His comfort!

> **"Blessed be the God and Father of our Lord Jesus Christ, the Father of mercies and God of all comfort, who comforts us in all our affliction, so that we may be able to comfort those who are in any affliction, with the comfort with which we ourselves are comforted by God." (2 Cor. 1:3–4)**

We weren't made to walk alone. We were made to run to Him every day.

Every single day

Don't try to tackle all that is coming at you by yourself.

Stop.

Sit at His feet.

Watch Him settle you, calm you, direct your steps, multiply your time, change your perspective, and give you peace.

Real peace

There is nothing you will face in this day that is too hard for Him.

Nothing

Oh, friend, *run* to *Him*; run to Him in His Word and in prayer, and then run to Him again tomorrow.

He will carry you.

He has you.

He loves you.

Forever

And these are the reasons we keep praying and seeking Him through His Word, day after day, all the way home.

Will you stop and pray?

Open your Bible to 2 Corinthians. Please pray and read Chapter 1.

36 *day thirty-six*

Please pray and reread 2 Corinthians 1:1–11.

Did Paul shake his head in frustration?

Paul had sent his first letter to the wayward church at Corinth, and early reports were that good changes were being made.

But then what?

A few months passed, and Titus brought word to Paul that false apostles in the church of Corinth were accusing Paul of all sorts of non-Christlike behavior.

Paul had suffered so much. He had dedicated his life to the cause of Christ. And he was being falsely accused of things exactly opposite of what he had been preaching.

This had to hurt—deeply.

But Paul put pen to papyrus once again. His second letter was personal, and it was passionate.

God would use it to correct, instruct, and strengthen His Church—both at Corinth and today.

Make no mistake, these words of 2 Corinthians are meant for our hearts—to be taken personally and applied to our lives.

Right off the bat, Paul said that the God of all comfort had comforted him in his afflictions. (2 Cor. 1:3)

And Paul intimately knew affliction—mentally, physically, spiritually, and emotionally.

He knew it in the very moment he wrote those words—as those he loved were believing lies about him.

His consolation in that moment and every moment was Christ. Paul wanted every believer to know that Christ is and always will be the greatest of all comfort.

And I have to stop there and ask myself: what have I run to for comfort just this past week?

Romantic love?

Financial security?

Order in my home?

Praise from others?

Appearance?

Health?

Career status?

A happy family?

Every single one of those things is fleeting and subject to change.

Even good things can be sinking sand if that's all we are leaning on.

But God

He is the Solid Rock.

Paul wanted the believers to truly know there is steadfastness to be had, regardless of circumstances. (2 Cor. 1:7)

And then Paul spoke the hard truth that this "steadfastness"—this continual habit of standing on the Rock of all comfort—is learned from suffering.

Suffering

What?!

That kind of preaching won't draw a crowd!

But it's the truth, and Paul knew it had to be taught.

There is a lesson to be had when we suffer. It is then that many come to realize we can't trust in things—even good things—to never fail us.

It is most often through suffering that we learn we can't even trust ourselves. But we can always trust in God. (2 Cor. 1:9)

Always

Daily living in this trust, over and over, is the game changer.

And, oh, how Paul had lived it! He exclaimed:

> **"We were burdened beyond measure, above strength, so that we despaired even of life." (2 Cor. 1:8b NKJV)**

Things had gotten so bad that he had wanted to die.

I hope you won't miss the honesty of this. The Bible is real. It is not sugar-coated fluff. God knows our lives can be hard and that sometimes we don't want to live. Our Father purposefully inspired Paul to include this despair. Then He stirred Paul to explain that hard times are for a purpose:

> **"Yes, we had the sentence of death in ourselves, that we should not trust in ourselves but in God who raises the dead, who delivered us from so great a death, and does deliver us; in whom we trust that He will still deliver us . . ."**
> **(2 Cor. 1:9-10 NKJV)**

God will deliver His children; He always has. We can trust Him.

And I know that. I believe that.

But *still*, my heart needs to be reminded again.

Let me be honest. I've stood on God's promises. I've held on to Him through some gut-wrenching times, but I've also been a crumpled mess when I've gone back to trying to rely on myself or anything else but Him.

And like those Corinthians who needed a *second* letter . . . so does my soul.

My wayward heart needs to be reminded, once again, that God is the God of all comfort, and I can continue to trust Him more than I trust myself.

And that is some truth to hold on to!

That is some steadfastness for a world full of sinking sand!

Oh, God's Word is so good!

37 *day thirty-seven*

Let's take a pause.

Yesterday, I picked up Paul's second letter to the Corinthians, asking God to teach my heart.

But I had to set it down, for I knew I had to follow God in what He had already taught before I could go one step further with Him.

And I think this is worth mentioning in case some of you need to spend some time allowing the Lord to examine your hearts before asking Him to help you move forward with this study.

For weeks, I had felt anger simmering in my soul. I tried to tap it down. I tried to ignore it. But it was there.

As you may know, my first husband took his life when my boys were just one and three. I have written a book about this (*Truth to Hold On To*), and I have shared my testimony on stages and radio programs.

But as is the case with suicide and many other wounds we face in this life, the effects are long-lasting, and the victims are many.

As I prayed, I realized that while I had forgiven Rick for leaving us, I also needed to forgive him for the pain my boys still deal with today.

So I drove to the cemetery—because where else do you go to forgive a dead person?

I cried again. I prayed again. I probably looked a little crazy as I stood there because I can't cry and pray without moving my hands.

But again, I gave God what I couldn't carry.

I've forgiven Rick again. I've asked God to use what the enemy intended for evil for good—again.

And now, I find I can raise my hands a little higher in worship; my heart feels a little freer because some chains have fallen back off.

And I wonder, is there anything holding you back from worship? Is there anything keeping you from all God has for you?

I don't know about you, but I don't want anything coming between the Lord and me.

Nothing is worth that!

I want to hear God's voice as clearly as I can so I can continue to grow closer to Him, love others well, and just plain *rest* in Him.

He is so good at showing us the way to do just that.

Will you spend some time this morning praying and asking our gracious Father to show you anything you need to give Him in order to walk forward in the new things He wants to teach you? Thank Him that He will show you—for your good and His glory.

38 *day thirty-eight*

Please pray and reread 2 Corinthians 1:12–24.

Remember, Paul had been falsely accused of selfish, impure motives.

He had given so much for the cause of Christ, and he defended his actions as sincere and not driven by fleshly, worldly wisdom—the things this world says matter. (2 Cor. 1:12)

Despite being misunderstood, Paul's goal remained for others to follow Christ and glorify God, and that was all Paul desired to boast in. (2 Cor. 1:14)

And suppose that is truly our goal as well. In that case, we, too, can confidently keep on pointing to Jesus when we are misunderstood, falsely accused, unappreciated, alienated, and persecuted by this world.

And we know that all of us who seek to follow Christ will have troubles. (John 16:33)

Serving Jesus is certainly not for the faint of heart. It was far from easy when Paul did so, and it is far from easy today. I suspect it will only get harder.

But for those who have tasted the goodness of the Lord, we are compelled to be disciples, regardless of how others might perceive us.

We must stand firm in our faith and speak the truth in love.

Our ears need to be tuned to the Holy Spirit's guidance, and our feet must be firmly planted in the Word. We need to remember that God will equip us for every good work He has called us to do. (Heb. 13:21; 2 Tim. 3:17) He is and will always be the source of our strength. (Eph. 3:16–19)

Our job is just to stay connected to Him and let His truth flow through us in love. On our own, we've got nothing worth giving or saying.

But because of Jesus, because we owe Him everything, because we want others to trust and follow Him, and because He deserves all honor, glory, and praise—because of *all* of that—we really don't have to be understood, liked, or well-treated by this world to keep on singing His praises!

Will you read that last sentence again?

Do you truly believe that? Perhaps you want to believe it but need God to help you. Remember, you can say to your Father, "I believe. Help my unbelief." God told us this was okay by including the account in Mark. (Mark 9:24)

I'm so thankful God gave us His Word and helps us believe it and live it!

39 *day thirty-nine*

Please pray and read 2 Corinthians Chapter 2.

Paul's motivation in confronting sin in those wayward believers at Corinth was the abundant love he had for them. (2 Cor. 2:4)

And when we love others, we are sometimes called to speak the truth about sin in their lives—and those who love us should speak it to us.

But after the believer has turned from his or her sin, we are to let it go.

Let it go.

Who are we to hold it against them?

What's more, when we define someone by his or her past sins, we are playing into the devil's schemes.

Paul said that we should "not be outwitted by Satan; for we are not ignorant of his designs." (2 Cor. 2:11) A NKJV commentary says, "One of Satan's chief devices is to cheat the believer from true forgiveness."

If the enemy can get us to define another believer by his past sins, that person may begin to define himself that way, too, and may very well fall back into those same sins again.

If God remembers our sins no more, why should we remember the sins of others—or even our own?

Let us, instead, help each other remember what Paul wrote a bit later in this letter:

> **"We are new creations in Christ." (2 Cor. 5:17)**

If we remind each other that God removes our sin as far as the east is from the west, then we can help each other keep walking as Christ defines us—not as the enemy would like to do so. (Psalm 103:12)

And maybe, somebody somewhere needs you to remind them today—or you may need to remind yourself—that those demons that knocked us down before are no match for the God inside us.

Because of Jesus, there is victory for all who call on His Name!

And that is a powerful thing!

(C.S. Lewis wrote an incredible book called *The Screwtape Letters* to help us "not be ignorant of the enemy's designs." I highly recommend it!)

40 *day forty*

Please pray and reread 2 Corinthians 2:12–17.

> "But thanks be to God, who in Christ always leads us in triumphal procession, and through us spreads the fragrance of the knowledge of him everywhere. For we are the aroma of Christ to God among those who are being saved and among those who are perishing, to one a fragrance from death to death, to the other a fragrance from life to life." (2 Cor. 2:14–16a)

The Corinthians would have understood this analogy because they would have seen victorious Roman generals leading triumphant armies and their captives. Priests would have carried censers filled with incense behind the conquering generals.

That aroma would remind some of victory and some of the chains of death.

As believers, God is indeed always leading us in triumphal procession. We need to remember that we are in a place of victory.

The battle has been won. We are just walking home!

We need to see our circumstances from that perspective. We must encourage each other to breathe in the sweet smell of victory. We are to be the aroma of Christ to each other.

But we also need to understand that to the lost world, we smell of death.

And, sometimes, those who don't call Jesus Lord will push us away because they don't want to be reminded of what they know we believe to be their future—death and Hell.

Deep down, those who are lost suspect that the God we are following really does exist and truly has the victory, but they aren't prepared for what they think surrendering to Him means.

That's one reason why they need to see our joy! Our King is worthy of our celebration—and not just at Christmas or Easter!

Our Christianity should be contagious!

As we understand our position in this triumphal procession to our eternal home and realize how the lost world sees this, we can sense an urgency for their souls while simultaneously and patiently loving them and living with joy among them.

May we remember we are following the triumphant King! We are already in the place of victory. God has won the battle, and our job is simply to follow Him home.

What a Savior!

41 *day forty-one*

Please pray and read 2 Corinthians 2:17 again.

> **"For we are not, as so many, peddling the word of God; but as of sincerity, but as from God, we speak in the sight of God in Christ." (2 Cor. 2:17 NKJV)**

In many of the Apostle Paul's letters, he warned of false teachers. False teachers were rampant in Corinth. They peddled the Word of God for their own profit.

There are still false teachers today. Our hearts must be on guard.

We must test everything we see and hear with God's Word.

Are those we listen to preaching the entire Word of God for our good and God's glory? Do they ever speak the hard things—like surrendering and dying to self? Or are they grace-heavy and truth-light?

Some stand on stages and only speak what our itching ears want to hear so that we will praise them and flock to them instead of God. (2 Tim. 4:3)

We have to test everything with God's Word, which is our standard of truth. With it, we can discern these things.

But we also have to test what our own hearts do with praise that comes our way— even ministry praise.

We were meant to reflect glory to our Lord, not try to absorb it. We can't handle the glory that belongs to the Lord, and it will burn us up if we try to reflect it upon ourselves.

John warns us that some will love the praise of men more than the praise of God. (John 12:43)

And our human hearts can make a stage out of absolutely anything—leading Bible study, our parenting, our jobs . . . and the list goes on.

We are *all* capable of getting drunk on the praise of others.

We can start to enjoy the influence and power that admiration brings.

We have to guard our hearts and minds in Christ Jesus with all diligence. (Prov. 4:23)

No, none of us can handle the glory that was meant for God. We will misuse it. And it will eventually own us.

But instead, may the meditation of our hearts—what we think about and what motivates us—and the words of our mouths be acceptable to our God. (Psalm 19:14)

And may we live our lives to praise the One deserving of all praise—for without Him, we would not even have our next breath.

What a Savior!

42 *day forty-two*

Please pray and read 2 Corinthians Chapter 3.

Fear is a liar. But what is fear's great lie? That God really won't be enough for me. But God said:

> **"Fear not, for I am with you; be not dismayed, for I am your God; I will strengthen you, I will help you, I will uphold you with my righteous right hand." (Isa. 41:10)**

That verse came to my mind many years ago as I lay pleading with the Lord the night I learned my first husband had taken his life. In my most fearful moment, God slayed my fears with truth.

Powerful truth
Hold-on-to truth
Fear-killing truth

Paul wrote about that truth and lived in that truth. He knew the truth that, no matter what this life brings, Christ is enough for us.

If Christ is truly sufficient—if He is truly enough for us—we have incredible hope! (2 Cor. 3:5, 12)

And that hope brings a boldness to live our lives without fear.

If Jesus is my everything, I can love others regardless of how they love me back—because Jesus has already filled my tank. He is my first love.

Because Christ is my prize, I can risk what others think of me to follow Him, even when the world is not. His praise is all I've learned to need.

Because of God's abiding presence, I can face the unknown, serve in the hard places, and let go of every earthly thing—because I know that on the other side of all I could ever face is my sweet Lord.

> **"Such is the confidence that we have through Christ toward God. Not that we are sufficient in ourselves to claim anything as coming from us, but our sufficiency is from God, who has made us sufficient to be ministers of a new covenant, not of the letter but of the Spirit. For the letter kills, but the Spirit gives life." (2 Cor. 3:4–6)**

And if Christ is enough for us, then we can keep going when the hard days come.

But you can't just take my word for it.

Open up His Word. Ask God to speak.

The same God who whispered that hope-giving truth from His Word during my tragedy will speak to you. He will comfort you.

Ask Him to remind you of His faithful love. Ask Him to calm your fears and guide your steps. Ask Him to help you be aware of His abiding presence.

Oh, He loves *you*! He loves you! He wants to make His nearness known in your life.

He wants you to trust Him and walk with Him in a real relationship.

Oh, how God has blessed me with many people and things I love since that tragedy came into my life all those years ago. He has used those broken days. He has restored my joy.

But all those blessings are just icing on the cake. God is my "cake." He is enough—more than enough. My hope and my confidence are in Him.

And when my knees get shaky, when I feel my strength failing, and even when I'm faithless, He is still faithful. (2 Tim. 2:13)

Every day
Every moment

> "Not that we are sufficient of ourselves to think of anything as being from ourselves, but our sufficiency is from God . . ." (2 Cor. 3:5 NKJV)

And for that, I am so very thankful. Aren't you?

Deep down, those who are lost
suspect that the God we are following
really does exist and truly has the victory,

*But they aren't prepared for
what they think surrendering
to Him means.*

43 *day forty-three*

Please pray and reread 2 Corinthians Chapter 3.

I don't know if it originated with him, but I can still hear Dr. Doug Sager say, as only he could, "Anytime you are reading Scripture and see "therefore," you need to ask what it's there for!"

And my eyes landed again on 2 Corinthians 3:12 (NKJV) this morning:

> **"Therefore, since we have such hope . . ."**

I asked myself what that hope was "there for."

Why? Why did Paul say there was "such hope"?

In the verses before, Paul described the new covenant. (2 Cor. 3:4–11)

Because of Jesus and the new covenant, everything has changed—both in this life and eternally.

But even though we *know this*, we have to fight to remember it and walk in the truth of the "such hope" that we have as Christians.

This temporary world has a way of consuming us. Christians, just like everyone else, get distracted and often discouraged. We sometimes forget the eternal "such hope" we have. We sometimes forget to look up from our circumstances to our Savior and remember we are never, ever without hope!

And that's one more reason we must soak in the truth from God's Word every day. I am so thankful to be able to study the Word every day. Aren't you?

Every day
Because my heart is prone to wander
Because my knees can get shaky

So let's help each other slow down and savor it. We need to get that truth in us.

And as we do, we find ourselves strengthened daily. We feel our hearts encouraged, and we discover this "such hope" flowing out from us into the lives of others.

Paul said that this hope caused him to speak with great boldness. (2 Cor. 3:12)

What Paul remembered to be true impacted his thoughts and actions.

And I don't know about you, but I need to remember the truth every day. I need to pick it up again and again—and not just for me. I pick it up for those I love.

My kids need me to remember the hope and walk in it. My husband also needs me to. Those people down the street and the ones I will meet next year need me to as well.

This "such hope" was meant to flow in and through us.

This is how we encourage one another—and all the more as we see the Day approaching. (Heb. 10:25)

Oh, friend, in this moment, our eyes may see the trouble around us. Jesus told us we would all face it, but as we read the Word—as we remember what He has told us—we can have peace.

> **"I have said these things to you, that in me you may have peace. In the world you will have tribulation. But take heart; I have overcome the world."**
> **(John 16:33)**

He gave us the Word so that we can have peace.

44 *day forty-four*

Please pray and read 2 Corinthians Chapter 4.

It's another "therefore" to wonder what it's there for:

> **"Therefore, since we have this ministry, as we have received mercy, we do not lose heart." (2 Cor. 4:1 NKJV)**

Paul had been talking about the new covenant—that because of Jesus, we have such hope. (2 Cor. 3)

He then expounded on it in 2 Corinthians 4, explaining that because of what Jesus has done—because we have received mercy and have a ministry—we don't "lose heart."

And *all* who have received Christ and His mercy most certainly have a ministry. (Remember, there is this thing called the "Great Commission" in Matt. 28:19–20.)

We are all called to be light in the darkness and shine our light so others will give glory to the Father. (2 Cor. 4:6 & Matt. 5:16)

So how are we to go about being the light of Christ in this dark world?

Oswald Chambers, the author of *My Utmost for His Highest*, asked, "Is your relationship with God sufficient for you to expect Him to exhibit His wonderful life in you?"

Basically, are you living in such a way that others can see Jesus in you?

Seriously, can those you know, those you work with, and those around you even tell you love Jesus? Or have you "lost heart" and given in to looking like the darkness around you? Paul said:

> **"We have renounced the hidden things of shame." (2 Cor. 4:2)**

So Paul is reminding us once again to take a sobering look at our lives and ask ourselves if we are accommodating sinful things—because sin can make us "lose heart."

Some are still playing with sin instead of fleeing it. Let us be warned.

If we don't take sin seriously enough, we will make the mistake of measuring ourselves against the lost world and conclude we are doing well. Paul later wrote that this is not wise. (2 Cor. 10:12)

But if we turn our eyes to the Lord—not once but often—and if we look to His holiness as our standard, we will find things in our lives that may not need to be there . . . that aren't bringing God glory.

So let's take a moment and prayerfully ask God to examine our lives and show us any hidden things of shame that need to be renounced.

Let's ask Him to examine everything—our entertainment, our language, how we treat others, what we run to for praise, and how we spend our time and money. Let's hold nothing back. Let's seriously take some time to be quiet and still before the Lord and ask Him to examine our hearts and show us any wicked way in us. (Psalm 139:23–24)

Let's also remember that when God shows us sin in our lives, it is out of His goodness because He has better things for us and better things to do through us. (Rom. 2:4)

Let's renounce the sin He shows us and live in such a way as to expect God to exhibit Himself through us.

When we live this way, we are truly living like we were made to live—giving glory to the One who saved us!

And that is truly living!

> "For it is the God who commanded light to shine out of darkness, who has shone in our hearts to give the light of the knowledge of the glory of God in the face of Jesus Christ." (2 Cor. 4:6 NKJV)

What a Savior!

Jesus has done
what we can never do for ourselves;
He has made every
problem
we will ever face in this world
temporary.

45 *day forty-five*

Please pray and reread 2 Corinthians 4:7–15.

We desperately need to be reminded of the hope we have. This letter to the church of Corinth was Holy Spirit inspired and is so full of hope for our hearts.

Why? Why do we need to read of hope when we've been saved by the blood of the Lamb? Because we aren't home yet. On this side of Heaven, our flesh forgets. Our souls become downcast. Our eyes forget to look beyond the here and now.

We struggle to remember God can make a way when our limited imaginations can't fathom any possible way.

And we who possess eternal hope often spiral down as if we have none.

Do you know what I am talking about?

But then the Holy Spirit inside of us reminds us of eternal truth. Oh, God, give us ears to receive it and hearts to hold on to it.

Doesn't your heart leap for joy when you read the words God had Paul write for your heart today?

> **"But we have this treasure in jars of clay, to show that the surpassing power belongs to God and not to us. We are afflicted in every way, but not crushed; perplexed, but not driven to despair; persecuted, but not forsaken; struck down, but not destroyed . . ." (2 Cor. 4:7–9)**

Oh, friend, hard things will come in this life, but our goal cannot be peaceful circumstances. To be sure, there will be moments this side of Heaven where all feels right in our world . . . but they are only temporary glimpses of what is to come.

We have to lay down our need to hold on to what can't be held on to in this life. We must lay down our idols of circumstantial comfort and peace.

We are jars of clay—we will be chipped and cracked and even broken—but as Paul said:

> **"We have this treasure in jars of clay . . . always carrying in the body the death of Jesus, so that the life of Jesus may also be manifested in our bodies."**
> **(2 Cor. 4:10)**

Because Jesus defeated death, nothing in this life can defeat those who call Him Lord, not even death.

Because we have eternal life, we have eternal hope—a surpassing power that is of God, not of us—that cannot be destroyed by any earthly trouble.

If our goal in our Christianity is for God to fix our temporary lives on this Earth just like we would have Him so we can experience peaceful circumstances all the time, we will be repeatedly disappointed.

His ways are not our ways. (Isa. 55:8–9)

But if our desire is to allow God to shine through our troubles, trials, and brokenness, then we will find the "such hope" that Paul wrote about.

> **"For we who live are always being given over to death for Jesus' sake, so that the life of Jesus also may be manifested in our mortal flesh." (2 Cor. 4:11)**

These trials that perplex us, these persecutions that frustrate us, and these times we have been struck down and think we can't get up are the greatest opportunities for others to see Jesus in us. May they be for the glory of God. (2 Cor. 4:15)

And these hardships are also, often, the most significant opportunities to remember for *ourselves* the treasure and surpassing power that He who raised the Lord Jesus will also raise us. (2 Cor. 4:14)

He will raise us!

Jesus has done what we can never do for ourselves; He has made every problem we will ever face in this world temporary.

So while this day may bring trouble, we are still walking toward home in powerful victory because of Jesus.

Oh, let's hold on to that! Let's remind each other of that! Let's walk forward in that!

What a Savior! What a *powerful* Savior!

Because we have eternal life,

we have eternal hope

a surpassing power that is of God,
not of us—

*that cannot be
destroyed by any
earthly trouble.*

46 *day forty-six*

Please pray and reread 2 Corinthians 4:16—slowly. Savor it.

> **"So we do not lose heart. Though our outer self is wasting away, our inner self is being renewed day by day." (2 Corinthians 4:16)**

And with those words, I remembered what God laid on my heart a few years back.

I had stood looking in the mirror, trying to pull out yet another wild, gray hair, when I realized I couldn't see the thing without my reading glasses!

However, I did notice that I could clearly see the deep wrinkles on my forehead and around my eyes, even without my new readers. Where have the years gone?

My hysterectomy has cured my hot flashes, but I now know the meaning of muffin top—and I don't mean the yummy kind you can buy at the bakery!

To tell you the truth, I could almost be distracted by my aging body if it weren't for my rapidly changing life. It seems my kids have grown up without even asking my permission—in the proverbial blink of an eye—and are leaving my nest.

No one asked me if I was ready for all of this or properly warned me it was coming. I do admit I totally ignored all those folks that said, "Your kids will grow up so fast."

I'm not prepared, and my retirement account isn't ready for the number of candles on my cake either!

If you gave me a few more moments, I could list many more things that, if I'm not careful, could tempt me into hosting my own pity party, like aging parents soon to be in need of more help, aches and pains in diverse places, a husband complaining of a balding head and nose hairs (what?), and many more life changes!

I can laugh at some of it, but to be honest, I could also cry. I feel really sad—the sadness that a good cry might help, but only temporarily.

As I lay in bed the other night, I began talking to my Father over the sound of my sweet husband's increasing-with-age snores. I began telling God how I felt: "I am not ready for my kids to be so grown-up and on their own. I even miss the chaos of little muddy feet and balls being thrown in my house. I miss holding them. I wonder just how far away they will move, and though I am happy for all of their opportunities, I miss them."

I know God has been faithful in the past, but can He help me with this sadness and this new host of emotions? Will He truly "renew me day by day"? Or is that just a pretty religious saying? (2 Cor. 4:16)

As I lay there in the dark, it hit me . . . God isn't just the God of "He did" or "He is." He is also the God of "He will" and "He can."

He hasn't taken away the emotions. He hasn't shown me how we will walk together in joy in this new phase of life. But He has assured me that He is already there, He is enough for my sad momma heart, and He will help me rest. He said:

> **"Come to me, all you who are weary and burdened, and I will give you rest."**
> **(Matt. 11:28 NIV)**

And so, each day, I'll just keep going back to Him with every emotion. I will pray for every care as my emotions bump up and down.

And although women often get stuck with the title of the "emotional ones," God chose to tell us about one of His men with a few up-and-down emotions. In Psalm 13, David wrote:

150

> **"How long must I wrestle with my thoughts and day after day have sorrow in my heart? How long will my enemy triumph over me?" (Psalm 13:2 NIV)**

When David wrote this, his enemies were encamped around him. He was depressed and afraid, and in his mind, he wrestled with his fears. But get this: only after telling God of his worries did David's emotions shift!

David found a prayer for every care!

David ended the Psalm by saying:

> **"But I trust in your unfailing love; my heart rejoices in your salvation. I will sing the Lord's praise, for he has been good to me." (Psalm 13:5–6 NIV)**

Once again, God used His Word to encourage me and show me how to find hope and rest despite my sadness. He wants to do this for all His children.

In these few short verses in Psalm 13, we see a prescription for battling the thoughts and worries that overcome us:

1. Give your burden to God. Tell Him what you are worried about in prayer.

2. State your trust in God, and focus on His character and capability—not on your problem, not your character or inability, and not on the way you feel at the moment.

3. Realize that your ultimate salvation is already secure. The most important battle is already won, and problems and emotions—both real and perceived—will not always plague you.

4. Remember God's faithfulness in the past, and praise Him because He will not forsake you in the future either. Trust that He will give you rest.

And so the God of "He did" and "He is" is also the God of "He will" and "He can" for every emotion and every circumstance that will come our way.

And for what it is worth for my female friends: bangs cover a multitude of wrinkles.

47 *day forty-seven*

Please pray and reread 2 Corinthians 4:17–18.

If I'm honest, some days I wonder if the really hard days are worth it.

More than once, when the trouble around me feels deep, I've uttered, "Oh Lord, won't you just come on and get us."

But then, as He does so often—at just the right time, right when I need it—God will remind me of the truth in His Word with the very next verses I come to in my daily reading.

> **"For this light momentary affliction is preparing for us an eternal weight of glory beyond all comparison, as we look not to the things that are seen but to the things that are unseen. For the things that are seen are transient, but the things that are unseen are eternal." (2 Cor. 4:17–18)**

Paul had already faced horrific things when he wrote this second letter to the Christians in Corinth. He called his afflictions "light." Yet they seem far from light when he described them later in his letter:

> **"Five times I received at the hands of the Jews the forty lashes less one. Three times I was beaten with rods. Once I was stoned. Three times I was shipwrecked; a night and a day I was adrift at sea; on frequent journeys, in danger from rivers, danger from robbers, danger from my own people, danger from Gentiles, danger in the city, danger in the wilderness, danger at sea, danger from false brothers; in toil and hardship, through many a sleepless night, in hunger and thirst, often without food, in cold and exposure. And, apart from other things, there is the daily pressure on me of my anxiety for all the churches."**
> **(2 Cor. 11:24–31)**

Please feel the weight of those *hard* things that this *real* man truly endured.

Maybe let your eyes reread those words and imagine if those were your trials to remember.

But don't miss this: this completely human man who faced all these hard trials said our afflictions are "preparing for us an eternal weight of glory beyond all comparison."

Paul told us that it is all worth it!

It's worth it because the hardest things can bring an "eternal weight of glory beyond all comparison"!

Paul wanted to help us learn to see our trials from this perspective.

For if we can shift our focus from our temporary afflictions—from what is seen to what is unseen —there is an eternal glory to be had. (2 Cor. 4:18)

This refocusing is how "we will not lose heart." (Remember 2 Cor. 4:16?)

But don't forget, this recipe for hope is not a one-time action.

We have to *daily* shift our focus, often even moment by moment.

We have to deliberately turn our eyes upon Jesus in order to not lose heart and walk forward in hope.

This is a decision we have to exercise over and over because life is hard!

Our Christian walk is not a cakewalk. We may not be physically beaten, but we all get beat down. We get weary. Trouble feels like trouble. Pain hurts. It is gut-wrenching sometimes.

But God is a shield about us, our glory and the lifter of our heads. (Psalm 3:3) He uses hard things to bring good in this life that is truly but a breath! (Rom. 8:28 & Psalm 144:4)

Paul knew this to be true, and we can know it too. God gave us the same Holy Spirit He gave Paul!

The Holy Spirit reminds us of the truth that God really is doing bigger things than our eyes can see through the difficult things we are facing in this life. (Eph. 3:20)

Sometimes, those trials are for us . . . so we can learn to trust God more. Sometimes, those hard roads are so others can see Jesus in us.

But either way, we've got to hold on to Jesus. We have to hold on to the truth from His Word.

We believe Him, and then we keep believing Him.

As we take one day at a time—as we keep following Him in obedience and trusting that He will put all our days together—we can rest in the fact that He will bring about an eternal glory that really is beyond all comparison!

Oh, friend, your Father has you! He has all that concerns you! Hold tightly to Him!

48 *day forty-eight*

Please pray and read 2 Corinthians Chapter 5.

It's kind of weird looking through my friend list on social media sites like Facebook and realizing several have died in just the few years I've been on Facebook.

Do you notice this as well?

Life is so short! None of us are here forever. These bodies are all dying.

So that makes us all feel good, right?

But when Paul wrote of death, he said:

> **"We are confident, yes, well pleased to be absent from the body and to be present with the Lord." (2 Cor. 5:8 NKJV)**

Paul did not fear death. He truly looked forward to eternity with Jesus!

He called the Holy Spirit his "guarantee," and he lived like he was taking that to the bank every day! (2 Cor. 5:5)

And because of this confidence in the abiding, powerful presence of the Lord in his life, Paul said it was his aim to be "well-pleasing" to God. (2 Cor. 5:9)

Is that your aim today—really, truly? Is that your *big* goal for the day? I have to ask myself if it is mine.

Like Paul, we who are Christians have that same Holy Spirit inside of us. Shouldn't we feel the same?

Paul continued by saying:

> **"For we must all appear before the judgment seat of Christ that each may receive the things done in the body, according to what he has done, good or bad." (2 Cor. 5:10 NKJV)**

Paul was talking to believers when he explained that our lives on this Earth would be evaluated.

Hear this: we certainly can't work to earn our salvation, but we aren't intended to just receive such great a gift and do nothing with it. Think about the parable of the talents. (Matt. 25:14–30) What's more:

> **"For the love of Christ compels us, because we judge thus: that if One died for all, then all died, and He died for all that those who live should live no longer for themselves, but for Him who died for them and rose again." (2 Cor. 5:14–15 NKJV)**

God, through Paul, is very clear: we who have been rescued, are sealed with the Holy Spirit, and love Jesus are to no longer live for ourselves but for Jesus.

Period
No exceptions
No excuses

Jesus talked about those who make excuses in the parable of the great banquet, and the funny thing is that all of their excuses involved everyday good things, like work, home responsibilities, and marriage. (Luke 14:15–24)

Those who made excuses weren't caught up in sin; they were just super busy with life!

But those busy people didn't get a pass in Luke 14, and neither will any of us when we only concern ourselves with our lives and our stuff.

God is talking to hard-working, church-going people when He says in Revelation:

> **"I know your works . . . nevertheless, I have this against you, that you have left your first love." (Revelation 2:4 NKJV)**

Oh, friend, we can all get so busy in this life that just keeps speeding by.

But don't get so busy and distracted that you have no room in your schedule to think about living to please the Lord.

Is it our daily aim to please Jesus? Does it even cross our minds? Paul brought this up again and again because we all have hearts that are prone to wander and be distracted. For this reason, we need to evaluate our lives often with questions like:

- How are we impacting someone else for the Kingdom?
- Are we compelled to do so?
- Do others see Jesus in us? Do they want what we have?
- Are we concerned about where those around us will spend eternity?

Perhaps, take a glance at your friend list on Facebook.

How many have died? I don't know. But perhaps the better question is: how many will die? The answer is all of them—unless Jesus comes to get us soon! How many of them don't know Jesus?

Have you ever talked with any of them about the real hope you have because of Jesus?

Oh, let's not wait! Let's be compelled to share the good news that is the amazing love of Christ Jesus! Let's just remember we are simply "beggars telling other beggars where we found bread," as noted evangelist D.T. Niles said.

Let's not be too busy for that!

49 *day forty-nine*

Please pray and reread 2 Corinthians 5:12–19.

If the love of Christ compels me, I can no longer regard anyone according to the flesh. This reminds me of a story.

They knocked on our door, wanting to know if we had any work for them. Just twelve and fifteen, unable to drive yet, they had walked from a nearby trailer park to see my husband. He had befriended the boys a couple of years prior (because that's just what my man does if he encounters you), and we have seen them occasionally since.

They sat on our porch and talked with us about their families and homes; they explained that they thought we were rich. They remarked about our house, our vehicles, and our iPhones.

I chuckled to myself, realizing perceptions are so relative.

I wouldn't consider our family wealthy, but I could point to a few families I have evaluated based on their outward appearance, just as those boys had evaluated mine.

I often look at the outside, and I make assumptions. Sometimes, those assumptions are way off—and not just about financial status. Sometimes, I wrongly evaluate the heart of another based on outward appearances or things I've heard about them. I may look at how someone dresses, the job they have, or a whole host of other things and assume to know all sorts of things about them.

I "fill in the blanks" with my own preconceived ideas, and sometimes, I get it all wrong!

But God looks at the heart, and He sees things differently—and always accurately.

God sees His children through the cleansing blood of His Son.

He told us through Paul that if someone is in Christ, he is a new creation; the old things have passed away! (2 Cor. 5:17)

But flesh-filled me, I often look at others as if the past were still stuck all over them.

Unlike my flesh nature, God does not see us with our sins all over us because Christ took them to the Cross! (2 Cor. 5:19). Oh, hallelujah that He did!

So whom are we to call unclean that God has called clean? (Acts 10:15)

Are we to define people based on what our human eyes can see or what our ears have heard about their past?

I don't know about you, but I don't want to be judged that way. I know how far in the pit my sin has taken me. I know how much God has forgiven! If Christ looks at my heart instead of my outward appearance or my sin, who am I to look at another in any other way? Who am I to call new things old? (2 Cor. 5:17)

May we pray for God to give us eyes to see and hearts to love others as He does. May His love compel us to look deeper, love truer, and be a light to all those around us.

What a Savior!

50 *day fifty*

Please pray and read 2 Corinthians 5:20–6:1. Read it slowly. Soak it in.

My life has been affected by many who love Jesus, but when I think about it, my life has probably been most impacted by those who keep loving Him, even when it's hard.

I posted a while back on social media about having a headache. Lots of friends encouraged me, but what it took for my friend Eddie to post a note of encouragement brought tears to my eyes.

ALS had taken his ability to move or speak. He typed with the aid of software that "read" his blinks—one arduous letter at a time.

Eddie is with Jesus now, but his joy in Jesus was real—despite his physical pain all the way to his last days. Both he and his wife, Cerella, sought to encourage others to keep holding on to Him.

I think, too, of Shawn and Charlene. Shawn's heart is working only at a sliver of normal capacity. Their lives have been radically altered, and the future is uncertain. He was facing an upcoming surgery when my husband and I met them for dinner.

Shawn didn't spend much time at all talking about his heart problems. Instead, his face lit up as he told us about the Sunday School class he was teaching and how much God was teaching him as he studied.

As we talked further, Shawn told us that his grandpa had taught that same class into his late eighties.

Shawn explained that as his grandpa's body grew tired from three different bouts of cancer, he would find himself nodding off as he tried to study and prepare. So his grandpa decided he would no longer sit to study the Word but would stand the whole time, so he wouldn't fall asleep.

Can you imagine that sweet old man standing there with his Bible so he wouldn't miss what God wanted to show him in order to teach others?

Eddie, Cerella, Shawn, Charlene, and Shawn's grandpa are all ambassadors for Christ.

> **"Now then, we are ambassadors for Christ, as though God were pleading through us: we implore you on Christ's behalf, to be reconciled to God."**
> **(2 Cor. 5:20 NKJV)**

So what about us? "Now then," are we not also to be ambassadors for Christ?

There is a "now then" in that verse! There is a response due on our part for what Christ has done for us!

We are all to be ambassadors for Christ, as though God were pleading through us.

We aren't to receive salvation and get comfortably "stuck" there.

Nor should our afflictions keep us quiet; rather, suffering has a way of bringing glory to our God in a way little else can.

Yes, the love of Christ in us should compel us to tell others about our Lord as if God, Himself, were pleading through us. (2 Cor. 5:20)

Let's not receive the grace of God in vain; let's tell others of the great things God has done for us in the good days and the hard ones! (2 Cor. 6:1)

What a Savior! Glory to Him!

51 *day fifty-one*

Please pray and read 2 Corinthians 6:1–7:1.

Paul listed some hard things he had encountered as he sought to tell others about the Lord. (2 Cor. 6:3–10)

Paul was defending his ministry and basically saying that he had hung in there through hard things because God was his strength. Paul's goal was God's glory and their good.

Paul talked throughout Scripture about being imprisoned, being falsely accused, having his motives questioned, enduring sleepless nights, suffering in poverty and sorrows, and having his friends pull away from him. Please let yourself feel what these real situations Paul faced must have felt like.

But once again—even though misunderstood and falsely accused, even though he risked his own life—Paul didn't shirk away because things were hard. He kept preaching the truth, even when it was unpopular.

Paul was full of emotion—pleading as if God were pleading through him—when he said:

> **"O Corinthians! We have spoken openly to you, our heart is wide open. You are not restricted by us, but you are restricted by your own affections."**
> **(2 Cor. 6:11–12 NKJV)**

The Corinthian Christians were being drawn by their own affections to ungodly people and ungodly things that were hurting their walk with the Lord.

Paul told them not to be unequally yoked with unbelievers. (2 Cor. 6:14)

He was not telling them to isolate themselves from unbelievers—we know this from reading other parts of the Bible—but he was telling them not to compromise with evil things in this world.

Paul's words to those believers are also a reminder to us: we are each "the temple of the living God." (2 Cor. 6:16)

> **"Therefore, having these promises, beloved, let us cleanse ourselves from all filthiness of the flesh and spirit, perfecting holiness in the fear of God." (2 Cor. 7:1 NKJV)**

We have to take these words written with such emotion—spoken by God through Paul—seriously.

As believers, we carry the Holy Spirit inside of us all the time. Everywhere we go, in everything we do, we carry Jesus with us.

And this should impact every choice we make—the words we say, the entertainment we choose, the way we conduct our businesses, the relationships we pursue, and so on.

When our choices are not godly or our affections draw us toward unrighteousness, we may think we are free, but we are really restricting ourselves from the better things God has planned for us. (2 Cor. 6:12)

Oh, but when we remember we always carry Jesus with us—when we choose to follow Him instead of taking part in the evil of this world—it's there that we find peace, hope, and joy greater than our hearts could ever find elsewhere.

And it is there that others see Jesus in us!

As the Psalmist said,

> **"For a day in your courts is better than a thousand elsewhere. I would rather**

> be a doorkeeper in the house of my God than dwell in the tents of wickedness. For the LORD God is a sun and shield; the LORD bestows favor and honor. No good thing does he withhold from those who walk uprightly. O LORD of hosts, blessed is the one who trusts in you!" (Psalm 84:10–12)

What a Savior!

How blessed we are when we follow Him!

52 *day fifty-two*

Please pray and read 2 Corinthians 7:1–7.

▌ **"Outside were conflicts, inside were fears." (2 Cor. 7:5b NKJV)**

Right now, as I come to that verse, I truly see the conflicts around me. They are ugly and distracting. They are impacting my family—how I feel the fear.

It's been gripping.

But Paul said, "Nevertheless . . ."

Never
The
Less
God

No matter how I feel—no matter what I face—God is never the less.

▌ **"Nevertheless God, who comforts the downcast, comforted us . . ."**
(2 Cor. 7:6 NKJV)

And once again, as I pick up my Bible, God comforts *me* through His Word and through many of His children. You know, He sent Titus for Paul.

The prayers, Scripture, and songs from friends over the years have helped lift my downcast spirit from eyeing my circumstances so that I could refocus on my Father—the source of *all* comfort and strength. I am so thankful He helps us help each other.

He helps us remind each other that He is our *protector*, *defender*, and *provider*.

No matter where life takes us, He is there. (See Psalm 23, Psalm 121, and Psalm 139.)

The things that unsettle me about our world aren't "fixed." They are still there, but they sure do seem to shrink when I compare them to my *never-the-less* God.

Oh, friend, let's keep encouraging one another and all the more as we see the Day approaching! (Heb. 10:24–25) We must do it because we who seek to serve and praise the Lord have a target on our backs. Let's assume that everyone, in or out of ministry, needs encouraging reminders of what's true about our God.

If Paul needed a Titus to come his way and encourage him, I suspect we all do. Let's be that for one another.

What a Savior we serve!

His is the Kingdom! His is the Glory! His is the Name above all names!

53 *day fifty-three*

Please pray and read 2 Corinthians 7:8–16.

As Paul's pen continued in his second letter to the church at Corinth, he brought up his first letter to them (1 Corinthians).

That letter was hard and to the point. He didn't mince words. He pointed out sin. He called them on the carpet. He didn't sugarcoat.

And those Corinthians were brought to godly sorrow over their sin.

Paul rejoiced in that because their "sorrow had led to repentance." (2 Cor. 7:9)

They had been made aware of their sin and had turned away from those things and back to God. And there was rejoicing! This is the Gospel over and over in the life of the believer. Paul Tripp says, "As the gospel puts you in your place, it also puts praise in your mouth."

A good preacher friend once told one of my kids, "Salvation is one big decision followed by lots of daily decisions." And it's true. The life of a Christian includes turning from our sin and turning to God . . . again and again.

Though the Corinthians had turned to God in many things, they still needed to lay down their ways to God's ways in some other areas. There was more sin that needed to be addressed and more sin to be walked away from.

Like the Corinthians, sometimes those things we need to die to aren't so obvious to us while we are caught up in them. Sin is seductive. It's often fun . . . at least for a while. Our flesh will be vulnerable to it until the day we take our last breath on this Earth.

And no matter how long we've walked with Jesus, we better not get "too big for our spiritual britches" because not one of us is immune from a wandering heart. That's why we all need some truth-tellers in our lives. We need godly friends who have permission to "ruffle our feathers" over our sins. Truth-telling friends are the best kinds of friends—the ones who truly love us. Those friends know that:

> **"Godly sorrow produces repentance leading to salvation, not to be regretted; but the sorrow of the world produces death." (2 Cor. 7:10 NKJV)**

Yes, we need these kinds of friends, and we also need to be these kinds of friends. The goal is not to judge others to condemn them—that's never our job. The goal is to lovingly point others to truth and freedom when we see them stepping in sin.

James told us:

> **"My brothers, if anyone among you wanders from the truth and someone brings him back, let him know that whoever brings back a sinner from his wandering will save his soul from death and will cover a multitude of sins." (James 5:19–20)**

This is not a popular way to live. Our culture certainly doesn't promote truth-telling. It's not politically correct. The enemy daily seeks to keep our mouths shut when it comes to helping each other walk away from sin. Sadly, it's even becoming rare to hear sin called "sin" from many of our pulpits.

But if we truly care for each other, we will speak the truth and receive the truth so that we might walk in the joy that comes from obedience.

I don't know about you, but although it doesn't often feel great at the moment, I'm so incredibly thankful for those small group friends, Bible study friends, and Jesus-loving brothers and sisters who have loved me enough to speak the truth in my life!

Find some of those friends! Be that kind of friend! They are the best kind of friends—and the joy-filled kind of friends.

54 *day fifty-four*

Please pray and read 2 Corinthians Chapter 8. Pay close attention to verses 1–15.

What's to my advantage? Am I missing something??

The Apostle Paul was talking to a group of mature believers when he said:

> **"But as you abound in everything—in faith, in speech, in knowledge, in all diligence, and in your love for us—see that you abound in this grace also." (2 Cor. 8:7 NKJV)**

What grace? What was he talking about? What was Paul encouraging them (and us) to do?

He was imploring Christians to willingly give themselves to the Lord, no matter their circumstances. (2 Cor. 8:1–5)

Paul was urging them to keep the faith and continue doing good, regardless of how hard life got around them. He used the impoverished, persecuted Macedonian Church as his example. He seems to have suggested that if *they* could cheerfully give of themselves, then all believers could give, regardless of the circumstances we find ourselves in.

But giving is hard. Writing a check is hard. Giving of ourselves—our time, our energy, our conveniences, our comfort—is terrifically hard, perhaps harder than writing a check.

Ministering to others is messy. It's inconvenient. Oh, I might go on that foreign mission trip (a good thing), but please don't ask me to get involved with that needy, messed-up family down the street.

We will write a check to support the church budget (also a good thing), but we don't have time to meet regularly with a new believer needing discipleship or that kid from a single-parent home needing a godly man in his life.

I'm happy to share a Christian post on my social media, but please don't ask me to write a letter to that drug-addicted family member in rehab.

Yes, like many of you, I'm often willing to give—but only so much—of my time or my money and only under the right, convenient, comfortable circumstances. But today, more than ever, I'm thinking that's not quite all we who call ourselves Christ-followers are called to do. You and I are called to willingly give ourselves away because that's what Jesus did. We must do this even when our lives are busy or hard.

Paul went on to emphatically say that this giving away of ourselves is for our advantage. (2 Cor. 8:10) Does it strike you odd that Paul didn't say it was for the recipient's advantage—but for *ours*? Can it really be true that when I die to myself, I truly live? (Gal. 2:20) Can it really be true that when I refresh others, I'm the one refreshed? (Prov. 11:25)

God's Word and the example of our Savior tell me that it is true.

And so, once again, God's Word convicts, challenges, and encourages me. But if I just read it and walk away unchanged in how I live, it does not benefit me or anyone else.

As I continue to read Paul's letter, the words of James come to my mind again:

> **"But be doers of the word, and not hearers only, deceiving yourselves. For if anyone is a hearer of the word and not a doer, he is like a man who looks intently at his natural face in a mirror. For he looks at himself and goes away and at once forgets what he was like. But the one who looks into the perfect law, the law of liberty, and perseveres, being no hearer who forgets but a doer who acts, he will be blessed in his doing." (James 1:22–25)**

Oh, friend, let's love others and give of ourselves, regardless of—and especially—when our own lives get hard. There is always a blessing there! It's to our advantage!

55 *day fifty-five*

Please pray and reread 2 Corinthians 8:22–24.

Paul called Titus his fellow worker and partner. (2 Cor. 8:23)

They were close. They shared the same goal. Their hearts beat for the same Lord. Their eyes were fixed on the same prize—the glory of Christ.

And they surely understood the struggles with ministry. Did they shake their heads over the same frustrations? Did they remind each other that their battles weren't really against the people who came up against their ministries?

In the next chapter, Paul would talk of spiritual warfare and the weapons with which "we" fight. Did he especially think about Titus when he wrote the word "we"?

I wonder if Titus and Paul broke bread together and talked about ministry, people, and the enemy's attacks. I wonder if they shared stories of watching captives being set free, the lost being found, and those who were far away being brought near to the One who loved them so.

I wonder if they found in each other a deep friendship, a strong bond, that comes when you find another who so intimately and similarly seeks the things of God.

Ministry is often lonely. Just walking with Jesus in a crazy, corrupt world makes it easy to feel like an "alien and stranger" here.

But there are other aliens out there! As much as the evil one would have us feel all alone in our desire to live for Jesus, others are "fighting the good fight" too!

And just like Paul's heart was encouraged by Titus, our hearts need to be encouraged by others who get what it is like to serve Jesus daily when many choose to walk away. There are times we all get down and discouraged. There are times we get off track. There are times the battle is fierce, and we need to hear the voice of another remind us of the truth we know.

For years, I was so incredibly blessed to be prayed for and encouraged by my friend Karen Alexander-Doyel.

The joy of the Lord really was her strength. She fought the good fight, and she finished the race so strong. I miss her so much since the Lord took her home and her faith became sight!

I learned so much from her. Over and over, I truly saw Jesus in her. I watched her hold on when many would have given up. I watched her praise Jesus when many would have walked away. I saw her cling to the Word and diligently teach others to do so when it was physically hard for her just to get out of bed. Her heart was humble, and her love for Christ was genuine.

And as her cancer progressed, I saw true joy in this dear, dear friend. She said she wanted to praise Jesus all the way to the gates . . . and she did!

As much as my heart broke over saying goodbye to my friend, I knew that goodbye was only temporary.

And I know that one glorious day, I'll get to stand at the throne with my friend, and together we will behold the One she kept telling me and so many others to keep our eyes on in this life.

I'm so thankful God blessed my life so sweetly with Karen and others like her (like Becky and Suzanne). And I pray that He has helped you find these kinds of friends too. This life is hard, but oh, what a powerful blessing to find others who love Jesus and love you too!

56 *day fifty-six*

Please pray and read 2 Corinthians Chapter 9.

Some theologians believe Paul was being playful—perhaps even a bit jokingly sarcastic—in his "encouragement" to the Corinthians to not sow sparingly and to be cheerful givers. He may have been intentionally stirring them up.

Hebrews 10:24 says:

> **"Let us consider how to stir up one another to love and good works."**

Paul knew his audience. Paul knew he could give them a bit of a playful poke or even a sarcastic shot to help them move forward in doing good things.

And you know, we are to all spur one another on to good works. We are to encourage each other to move forward in doing good things, including giving our time and talents.

Paul's motivation to encourage the Corinthians, who may have been slack in giving to ministries with eternal impact, was for their own good.

Indeed, Paul's motive was for the good of others and the good of the ministry of Christ, and if this is our motive, then we can also feel free to encourage others to move forward. Like Paul, we want to do so with an understanding of who we are encouraging and by prayerfully considering what method of encouragement might work best for them.

As a word of caution, I have tried to spur others on without praying first for insight, and things did not go so well! However, in the times I have prayed before having those conversations, the outcome always went better.

And let's also remember that we need to cultivate friendships with others who have permission to give us a "soft kick in the can" when we need one—and we all need one sometimes.

Oh, friends, isn't the Word good and practical? Let's daily seek to apply it to our lives. Let's ask the Lord to examine our hearts when it comes to things like giving. Let's ask Him to help us graciously receive spurring on from others, and let's be prayerful in all our endeavors to encourage those we love.

57 *day fifty-seven*

Please pray and read 2 Corinthians Chapter 10.

I had been staring at 2 Corinthians 10 for two days. That powerful passage about our Mighty God and our weapons of warfare was especially timely as my heart had been begging to feel His nearness.

In the days before, I sat with my friend as she was dying. And I've listened to another friend whose heart was breaking over her prodigal. My heart felt so heavy over that and lots of other hard things.

As I was mulling all this over, several who follow me on social media—not knowing what I was going through—found and shared a post from several years ago about the supernatural nearness of our God.

I don't think any of this was a coincidence as I found myself trying to get a glimpse of the supernatural weapons with which we fight, described in Chapter 10 of 2 Corinthians.

Let me explain: this sort of supernatural thing has rarely happened in my life—maybe only once or twice. Here is the post that was re-shared that day:

I have heard God speak most often through His Word but rarely through such a supernatural, stand-in-awe, incredibly clear way as He spoke in the story I am about to tell you.

Several years ago, I woke up to a text from my brother telling me he was planning to drive up and spend the day with my parents. He lives about 45 minutes away, and it was highly unusual for my brother to miss his church on a Sunday.

He explained that as he had his early morning prayer time, he felt a strong sense of urgency to head our way. (We recently built a house for my parents beside our home because my dad is dealing with dementia.)

My brother said mom had mentioned she was not feeling well when he told her he was coming for a visit. I told him I thought my parents would love to see him, and I got ready to leave for church.

After church, I sat eating lunch with my kids at a restaurant when I received a phone call from my brother that my mom was throwing up blood.

Blood

I was only three minutes from the hospital—imagine that—and I told my brother I would meet them there.

I will spare you the nightmarish details of the next few hours, but I will tell you I have never seen so much blood. I can only explain it by saying it was like a horror movie as my mom was rushed to emergency surgery and ICU for a ruptured cluster of veins in her stomach, which was pouring blood into her stomach and spewing out her mouth.

My godly mother grabbed my hand in the midst of it all to tell me that if things didn't "go well," I would be okay because I knew where she would be. She would be with the God she had taught me about.

We almost lost my mother that Sunday night.

But God—the same good God—took care of us.

Normally on a Sunday morning, my parents would have been at their house (across the road from mine) with my family away at church. Because of my dad's dementia, he has forgotten how to use a phone. If he had run to my house, I would not have been home. He would have panicked, and my mom might have bled to death in front of him. How terrifying that would have been for them.

But God

He supernaturally pressed on my brother's heart to be with my parents that morning.

I am so thankful my brother was up seeking the Lord and listening for His voice—as he usually does early every morning and even on Sundays.

I am so incredibly thankful that we can trust God to make our paths straight when we acknowledge Him, even in supernatural ways like this.

Indeed, I know more than ever what this verse means:

> **"Trust in the LORD with all your heart, and do not lean on your own understanding. In all your ways acknowledge him, and he will make straight your paths." (Proverbs 3:5–6)**

God will direct your steps! God directed our steps!

Those who seek Him really do find Him. God told us in Jeremiah:

> **"You will seek me and find me, when you seek me with all your heart." (Jeremiah 29:13)**

My brother, day in and day out, seeks the Lord. That discipline has turned into devotion and deep trust over the years. And because my brother has trained his ears to hear the Lord, he knew that day that God was speaking and telling him to go and be with my parents.

I shudder to think about what would have happened if Chuck had not recognized the Holy Spirit, listened to Him, and acted.

I am so thankful for our Lord, who miraculously intervened to get my mother life-saving help and prevent a tragedy. God is real. He speaks. Friend, He will speak in your life too.

Are you listening for His voice?

Do you discipline yourself to be still, listen, and know that He is God?

Yes, sometimes He speaks in supernatural ways. But He always speaks through His Word. He wants to make His will known.

Isn't it amazing that God reminded me about His supernatural presence (by others resharing my previous social media post) on the very day that I was studying the supernatural weapons with which we fight?

All that to say, this effort you are putting forth into studying the Word, seeking God and His ways, oh, friend, it's worth it!

> **"But whoever listens to me will dwell safely, and will be secure, without fear of evil." (Proverbs 1:33 NKJV)**

And speaking of evil . . . let's talk more tomorrow about these weapons we have to fight with!

58 *day fifty-eight*

Please pray and reread 2 Corinthians Chapter 10.

They said he was bold with his letters and wimpy in person. They said he preached with impure motives to draw attention to himself. They said he was flesh-controlled rather than spirit-controlled.

These words had to cut especially deep, considering all Paul had endured bringing the good news of the Gospel to those who now falsely accused him or didn't defend him.

He was begging those in Corinth, whom he had called brothers and sisters, to deal with the false accusations before he arrived there. (2 Cor. 10:2)

And then he said those famous words—those words that embolden and encourage our weary hearts:

> **"For though we walk in the flesh, we do not war according to the flesh. For the weapons of our warfare are not carnal but mighty in God for pulling down strongholds, casting down arguments and every high thing that exalts itself against the knowledge of God, bringing every thought into captivity to the obedience of Christ, and being ready to punish all disobedience when your obedience is fulfilled." (2 Cor. 10:3–6 NKJV)**

Oh, friend, when trouble comes—and it will—our hearts can keep going when we remember our weapons are powerful and not of this world.

On a high hill overlooking ancient Corinth was a fortress. The Corinthians were all familiar with this sight, and Paul used this imagery when he confidently told them that strongholds could be pulled down. Arguments and every high thing that exalts itself against God will be cast down when we bring "every thought into captivity to the obedience of Christ."

As our thoughts are hedged in by the truth of the Word—which we must read daily—we find ourselves free from the lies of the evil one. We remember we have a future and a hope. (Jer. 29:11)

In fact, as you remember what God says about you, the lies of others have "no legs" to stand on and will fall to the ground. I know I am who He says I am—and so should you. Why? Because there is peace and power there!

Certainly, people may judge us by our outward appearances and the things they think they know about us. They may misunderstand us, not appreciate us, and even falsely accuse us and seek to harm us. (2 Cor. 10:7)

But we don't class ourselves or compare ourselves with those who commend themselves. (2 Cor. 10:12)

No! If we want out-of-this-world freedom, we have to get our eyes off others' opinions of us (good or bad) and their treatment of us, and we must focus on what God says is true about us.

We must get into the practice of doing this every day. We must go to the Word for truth. This is our "straight stick," as Spurgeon used in his analogy. When we take our thinking—which may be crooked and wrong—and compare it to the straight stick, anything that doesn't line up with the straight stick of the Word (the truth) is then refuted and discarded.

As we compare our thoughts with truth from the Word, day after day and year after year, we find ourselves walking in more and more peace. Yes, there may be days when we stumble and listen to the lies of the enemy. But as we remember the battle belongs to the Lord, and as we fight with spiritual weapons far greater than our flesh could ever muster on our own, we find the strength to walk away from the lies, and the Kingdom of God just keeps on advancing.

> **"But 'he who glories, let him glory in the Lord.' For not he who commends himself is approved, but whom the Lord commends." (2 Cor. 10:17–18 NKJV)**

We aren't glorying because we are walking better than others around us; we are glorying because we are following the Lord and His will for our good and His glory!

Oh, friend, let's live for His glory! When we keep our eyes on Him and live for Him, we can walk forward in powerful peace!

As our thoughts are hedged in

By the truth of the Word—

which we must read daily—we find ourselves free
from the lies of the evil one. We remember

*we have a future
and a hope.*

59 *day fifty-nine*

Please pray and read 2 Corinthians Chapter 11.

Believers today are no more immune from being led astray by false teachers than the early Church was. We are, perhaps, even more at risk. Paul spent much of Chapter 11 warning the Church about false teachers.

Since the beginning of time, angels of darkness have posed as angels of light. So don't doubt for a second that an all-out war is still being waged for the hearts and souls of men.

And to be sure, the fiery-dart lies of the evil one are aimed at our minds. God's Word tells us:

> **"As he thinks in his heart, so is he . . ." (Prov. 23:7 NKJV)**

There is a daily battle raging between our ears. If we can be convinced to call evil "good" and good "evil," we will quickly fall to all sorts of destruction. Again, this is why knowing the Word is so very important. The time you spend reading it will never return void and is more important than any word any human will ever write.

And those false teachers who pose as angels of light are smooth in their approach. They are alluring in their presentation. The lies they are selling seem attractive on the surface.

We are called to test all things and hold on to the good. (1 Thess. 5:21) But again, how can we know if something is false if we never study what is true?

If we never spend time on our own in the Word, we are nearly defenseless in our ability to discern.

If we only rely on what others tell us to be true about God and His ways, we may be easily deceived and drawn like flies to false teachers preaching an empty, worldly religion. But God's Word helps us know the truth.

Just before Paul began this portion of his letter about false teachers, he said:

> **"But he who glories, let him glory in the LORD. For not he who commends himself is approved, but whom the Lord commends." (2 Cor. 10:17–18 NKJV)**

And with that, we have some more truth to use to test what we hear and who we hear it from.

False teachers seek their own glory. They desire to draw people to themselves instead of God. They are often "grace-heavy" and "truth-light" in their speeches. And people with "itching ears" are drawn to their books, podcasts, and social media like flies. False teachers pick and choose parts of the Bible that make us feel good and leave out the truth that convicts and sets us free. They twist the Word in ways that support their false teaching.

Now more than ever—with social media blasting all kinds of lies and with nearly anyone able to attain a platform—we must diligently test everything we hear against God's Holy Word.

Oh, friend, let's hold tight to the truth. Let's spend time in the Word so we will be much better equipped to refute what is false and hold on to what is true.

60 *day sixty*

Please pray and read 2 Corinthians 11:22–33 and Chapter 12.

Have you ever pleaded, "God, why won't you take this away?"

Paul did.

Paul described the trials and hardships he endured for the cause of Christ—hard labor, imprisonments, beatings with rods, stoning, robbery, and multiple shipwrecks. He said he had been cold, weary, hungry, and without sleep. He had been betrayed by friends, misunderstood, and falsely accused. (2 Cor. 11:22–29)

And then Paul said an odd thing:

> **"If I must boast, I will boast in the things which concern my infirmity."**
> **(2 Cor. 11:30, NKJV)**

At first glance, it seems as if Paul might have been trying to prove his allegiance to Christ because of his endurance of hard things. To be sure, Paul didn't give up serving the Lord when he was persecuted for doing so.

But there is more.

Paul continued by talking of the thorn in his flesh that he had pleaded with the Lord to take away. Scholars still debate the nature of Paul's thorn. Regardless of the type of "thorn," we know it was a hardship that Paul had asked God to take away multiple times; but God had chosen not to do so for one of His most dedicated servants. (2 Cor. 12:7–8)

And with that "no," Paul could have stomped off, reasoning that surely God should remove his thorn with all he was enduring for Christ.

Can any of you relate?

Surely we can. How many times have I begged God just to fix something? How many times have I prayerfully explained and attempted to shamelessly "bargain" with Him that I could serve Him better if I didn't have to deal with that?

As Christians, we believe in an all-powerful God. And the more we walk with Him, the more we realize He will sometimes do things we don't like or understand. Often, our minds are tempted to reason that if our Heavenly Father truly cared about us, He would take away our painful troubles.

In fact, as believers, we know—we are certain—that with just a word from His mighty lips, our struggles could vanish. That's all it would take! Paul knew that too. He said:

> **"I pleaded with the Lord three times that it might depart from me."**
> **(2 Cor. 12:8 NKJV)**

Please feel the heaviness of those words. Paul was begging God to take "it" away.

But God said, "No." God had something better for Paul. Paul continued:

> **"And He said to me, 'My grace is sufficient for you, for my strength is made**
> **perfect in weakness.'" (2 Cor. 12:9a NKJV)**

Paul received God's perfect strength. And it is precisely there—in our weakness—that the power of Christ rests on us. (2 Cor. 12:9) In Paul's life, and in ours, weakness is, often, the very avenue through which God's power and purpose come. When we are stretched beyond ourselves—weary, worn, tempted, and tried—yet we give "it" to God to use for His purpose and His glory, we find a supernatural, keep-going peace!

We see His strength in us. We see Him fight our battles. We see Him provide a way. We see Him help us hold on. We see Him do in and through us what we could never do ourselves. This is God's perfect strength for us!

Knowing that God-in-you is carrying you through what you could never walk through on your own is so much more than some "pump-you-up" motivational speech. And it is there that the weakest of weak among us (like me) can, like Paul, say:

> **"For when I am weak, then I am strong." (2 Cor. 12:10b)**

Strong

We *can* be strong—whatever the thorn—because Jesus is with us, always faithfully with us.

And, like Paul, we can say:

> **"Therefore I will boast all the more gladly of my weaknesses, so that the power of Christ may rest upon me. For the sake of Christ, then, I am content with weaknesses, insults, hardships, persecutions, and calamities. For when I am weak, then I am strong." (2 Cor. 12:9–10)**

Content in the struggle of this day
Strong for whatever life may bring

Oh, friend, what a Savior! These aren't easy words, but they hold freedom-giving power. May He strengthen us to walk in whatever He calls us to. May we know that He is no less with us than He was with Paul.

God with us is enough!

The same God who strengthened Paul
will strengthen us in our weaknesses.

*He will ready us
for the battles.*

As we stay connected to the source of our strength—
as we follow Him even when others are
walking the other way—

*the Holy Spirit inside of us
will give us just what we need,
one day at a time.*

61 *day sixty-one*

Please pray and reread 2 Corinthians Chapter 12.

Are you willing to be "loved less" if that's what it takes?

Paul pleaded with the believers in Corinth to see his sincere love for them throughout his second letter to them. But as part of this "for-their-good" love, he was willing to be loved less by them. Sometimes, truly loving others requires us to be prepared to be disliked and even rejected.

Godly parents probably understand what Paul meant—think about those teenage eye-rolls—when he said:

> **"And I will very gladly spend and be spent for your souls; though the more abundantly I love you, the less I am loved." (2 Cor. 12:15 NKJV)**

Paul had encountered this "because-I-love-you" conflict with his "spiritual children" before and was prepared to face it again. Paul knew the goal could not change regardless of their response and said toward the end of his letter:

> **"But we do all things, beloved, for your edification. (2 Cor. 12:19b NKJV)**

The ESV says: "all for your upbuilding, beloved."

Paul's days were hard and often lonely. His efforts to bring the good news of the Gospel and teach others how to follow Christ brought him more and more hardships and true heartache. His journey on this Earth did not end "worldly-well." He was ultimately beheaded in Rome.

But in reading his letters, we know Paul believed it all to be worth it if others would come to know God and give Him glory. Like so many who were martyred for the faith, including all the disciples except John, Paul's goal was not to be right for pride's sake but that his words and actions would cause others to seek and follow God.

Friends, this must be our goal as well. We need to check our hearts on this, especially in this combative, mean-texting/posting/tweeting world.

Paul viewed every encounter—both good and bad—as an opportunity to exalt the name of Christ. This eternal perspective brought amazing contentment to Paul that far outweighed his earthly circumstances. By all accounts, Paul found genuine peace living out his God-given purpose—and so can we.

So Can We

The same God who strengthened Paul will strengthen us in our weaknesses. He will ready us for the battles. As we stay connected to the source of our strength—as we follow Him even when others are walking the other way—the Holy Spirit inside of us will give us just what we need, one day at a time.

But to be sure, what God gives us is never meant to be stored up for ourselves. It is to be poured out for the good of others and the glory of Christ.

A few years after Paul penned this second letter to the Corinthians, he found himself imprisoned in Rome. Though life had only gotten harder, Paul was still teaching with his eye on the prize and had the same heart as he wrote these words in his letter to the church at Philippi:

> **"Do all things without complaining and disputing, that you may become blameless and harmless, children of God without fault in the midst of a crooked and perverse generation, among whom you shine as lights in the world, holding fast the word of life, so that I may rejoice in the day of Christ that I have not run in vain or labored in vain." (Phil. 2:14–16 NKJV)**

Oh, friend, let's hold fast to the Word of life; let's shine our light. And one day, like Paul, may we rejoice over those children and spiritual children who've seen Jesus in us in this hard world.

Are you ready? Spend some time in prayer today, and ask the Lord to open your eyes to those around you who need godly encouragement—even if that encouragement may include saying the hard things. May the Lord give us a sweet boldness for His glory and the good of others!

If Jesus is your Savior,
it's absolutely a fact
that His Holy Spirit is in you!

62 *day sixty-two*

Please pray and read 2 Corinthians Chapter 13.

I'm a bit sad as I come to the end of Paul's letter to the church of Corinth. These holy words have convicted, challenged, encouraged, and comforted me. And these last words are no different.

Paul reminded the Corinthians (and us) that Jesus is not weak in dealing with us but is powerful among us. (2 Cor. 13:3) He is involved in our lives—in my life and your life—this very moment!

And not only that, do you realize that if you are a believer, Jesus is in *you*? (2 Cor. 13:5)

This is astounding truth! Maybe you've heard it before, but let's just soak it in for a moment.

It's mind-boggling and supernatural, but if Jesus is your Savior, it's absolutely a fact that His Holy Spirit is in you! And it is a truth you and I need to hold on to, living as if we actually believe it! Why? Because being aware of the nearness of God changes our behavior. This awareness of His holy presence impacts where we go, what we say, how we spend our time, what we think about, and on and on.

This awareness causes us to live as believers should live.

Paul said:

> **"Examine yourselves to see whether you are in the faith." (2 Cor. 13:5)**

Paul was not asking them if they were believers. Remember, he had been writing to Christians in Corinth. Instead, he was asking them if they were *living* like they were believers with an awareness that "Jesus Christ is in you." (2 Cor. 13:5)

So we who seek to know and follow God must ask ourselves the same thing—and often. Let's ask God daily to show us anything in our lives that is outside of His will. Let's train our ears to listen for His voice and let Him guide our actions and our words.

There have been moments when I've had absolutely no idea what to do or say, but as I prayed and listened, God gave me words that were clearly beyond my ability to think of or form.

Then there have been other times when I've tripped over my tongue, listened only to my own thoughts and fears, and said plenty of things I should not have said.

What's the difference?

In the first instance, I listened to the Holy Spirit; but in the latter, I ran ahead, or rather "talked ahead," in my own strength.

Luke recorded a time when Jesus was talking to His disciples about what they would say when questioned about their faith by government and religious leaders. He told them:

> **"Do not worry about how or what you should answer, or what you should say. For the Holy Spirit will teach you in that very hour what you ought to say."** (Luke 12:11b–12 NKJV)

Just as He did for the disciples, in the moment that we need it, the Holy Spirit will speak and give us what we need to do and say.

Our job is to listen for His voice.

His voice

Do you know it?

Can you hear it over your own thoughts and worries? And how do you know if what you are hearing is His voice? Well, for one, it will always align with God's Word, the Bible.

You can be sure that the Holy Spirit will never tell you to do or say anything that contradicts God's Word. This is yet another reason to be dedicated to studying Scripture.

In fact, one of the Holy Spirit's jobs is to remind us of what God has said:

> **"These things I have spoken to you while I am still with you. But the Helper, the Holy Spirit, whom the Father will send in my name, he will teach you all things and bring to your remembrance all that I have said to you." (John 14:25–26)**

And here is what Jesus said right after He said that (one of my favorite verses):

> **"Peace I leave with you; my peace I give to you. Not as the world gives do I give to you. Let not your hearts be troubled, neither let them be afraid." (John 14:27)**

Do you know what we can take from this?

There is freedom from worry and amazing peace to be had as we study the Word and train our ears to hear the voice of the Holy Spirit reminding us of truth—and as we say and do what He says!

Paul continued in this letter by saying:

> **"Now I pray to God that you do no evil . . ." (2 Cor. 13:7)**

Simply put: do what is right, not what is wrong. Listen for the voice of the Holy Spirit inside of you, and do what He says. He will not lead you into evil but in the way of peace.

Paul told believers to become complete by comforting one another, getting along, and living in peace. (2 Cor. 13:11)

Why these final words? Why this sum-up? Because when we live in this way; when we remember Jesus is in us, which means we take Him everywhere we go; when we examine ourselves and diligently follow Him and His ways; and when we seek to live in peace with others, we will experience the God of peace and love in our lives!

No, life won't always be a cakewalk. (Some of you are saying "Amen!" right now.)

But, oh, what a treasure of hope we have as believers!

63 *day sixty-three*

Please pray and spend a few moments looking back over 2 Corinthians.

As the Corinthians stood holding Paul's second letter, as his words came to a close, I wonder, did they turn back a few pages and reread to remember the treasure that comes from living our lives to follow Jesus?

This letter has been so very rich—so full of life-giving truth.

Did those early believers think about the eternal glory that awaited them as they looked over those Holy Spirit inspired words? Do we?

As you thumb back through your Bibles, what words did you underline? What treasures did you find? What hope? What comfort? What direction?

Hard days drew me to this letter, and I have found such hope through this slow savoring of it.

> **"So we do not lose heart. Though our outer self is wasting away, our inner self is being renewed day by day. For this light momentary affliction is preparing for us an eternal weight of glory beyond all comparison, as we look not to the things that are seen but to the things that are unseen. For the things that are seen are transient, but the things that are unseen are eternal." (2 Cor. 4:16–18)**

Oh, friends! Eternal glory awaits! Let's not lose heart! May we hold tight to the truths in this beautiful letter! May the Holy Spirit remind us of these powerful, hope-filled words at just the right time. He will do so, you know, just when you need them because that is what He does. (John 14:26)

And as we are reminded of truth, may we walk forward in the freedom that comes from following Christ! And may others see Jesus in us and be drawn to Him.

May Paul's final words to the church of Corinth be our words too:

> **"The grace of the Lord Jesus Christ, and the love of God, and the communion of the Holy Spirit be with you all. Amen." (2 Cor. 13:14 NKJV)**

May God's grace, love, and communion be with us all!

What a Savior!

AS WE CLOSE

There's something so wonderful about slowing down and reading the Word. It is a blessing we can count.

And you know, though our earthly blessings are fleeting, there are hints of Heaven in every one—how I want to hold tight to each of them.

But they are like soap bubbles blown from a wand; they shine and dance, float away, and are quickly gone.

I can't hold them in my hands. I can only hold them in my heart.

A white dress and a church aisle
A long kiss
My newborn baby lying on my chest
First smiles
First giggles
First "I love you, mommy"
Easter dresses
School plays
Friday night ballgames
Thanksgiving dinners
Christmas mornings

Crackling fires
Long talks
Long walks
Slow dances
Crunching fall leaves
Tiny snowflakes
First flowers of spring
Sunrises
Sunsets
Mountaintops
Babbling creeks

Porch swings
Lemonade on hot summer days
Cool breezes
Ice cream
White sand
Ocean waves
Fuzzy blankets
Hot coffee
Bathtubs

PJs
Laughter with close friends
Holding hands and praying
Sunday mornings
Church songs
Simple things
Little things
Good things
Blessings

Even—and especially—in the midst of heartache and hard days, may we see our blessings.

Let's count them and be reminded that not every day is a hard day. God gives us good days, fun days, and belly-laughing, joy-filled days too.

He is behind every blessing we can see and taste and feel. (James 1:17)

And the Giver of good things is working even hard things together for good for those who love Him, for those who are called according to His purpose. (Rom. 8:28)

Even the hard things we face in this life

Yes, we live in a fallen world, but we never, ever face one day of it alone. (Deut. 31:6)

Our Father is with us and with those we love.

He gives us the strength we need, when we need it, to walk through life's hardest moments. (Isa. 41:10)

The Apostle Paul sure knew this and wanted us to know it as well.

> "But we have this treasure in jars of clay, to show that the surpassing power belongs to God and not to us. We are afflicted in every way, but not crushed; perplexed, but not driven to despair; persecuted, but not forsaken; struck down, but not destroyed; always carrying in the body the death of Jesus, so that the life of Jesus may also be manifested in our bodies. For we who live are always being given over to death for Jesus' sake, so that the life of Jesus also may be manifested in our mortal flesh. So death is at work in us, but life in you. Since we have the same spirit of faith according to what has been written, 'I believed, and so I spoke,' we also believe, and so we also speak, knowing that he who raised the Lord Jesus will raise us also with Jesus and bring us with you into his presence." (2 Cor. 4:7–14)

Yes, weeping may last for a night, but joy comes with the morning. (Psalm 30:5)

The Word helps me remember that. It will help you too.

Yes, we've mourned, and we will likely mourn again before this life is over. I do not deny the hard in this world. But I've also flipped over to the back of The Book.

One day, our mourning will be forever turned into dancing!

One day, the blessings will be without end for God's children!

One day, all that is wrong will be made right forever!

One day, there will be a new Heaven and a new Earth!

Oh, how Paul must have had this in mind as he sought to encourage the body of believers through his letters.

But God didn't just give us Paul's letters. He gave us *all* of the Word. He gave us the Holy Spirit, who helps us remember hope just when we need it.

Oh, friend, as we come to the close of this devotional, I pray your hunger for the Word has only grown. I hope you know you can pick it up on your own, and every day you do so will yield blessings.

May we be ever more inspired to hold tight to the One who is coming again. May our hearts look forward to the words God gave John on the island of Patmos:

> **"Then I saw a new heaven and a new earth, for the first heaven and the first earth had passed away, and the sea was no more. And I saw the holy city, new Jerusalem, coming down out of heaven from God, prepared as a bride adorned for her husband. And I heard a loud voice from the throne saying, 'Behold, the dwelling place of God is with man. He will dwell with them, and they will be his people, and God himself will be with them as their God. He will wipe away every tear from their eyes, and death shall be no more, neither shall there be mourning, nor crying, nor pain anymore, for the former things have passed away.'" (Rev. 21:1–4)**

One day, the blessings won't seem to float away like soap bubbles. One day, the aroma of sweet anticipation won't fade.

One day, our faith really will become sight as it has for our beloved Paul.

One day, our eyes will behold what our hearts know is true.

Jesus
God with us
The greatest of all blessings
The Perfect Lamb

Our eyes will behold glory and blessings far beyond anything we can imagine forever and ever!

> "No longer will there be anything accursed, but the throne of God and of the Lamb will be in it, and his servants will worship him. They will see his face, and his name will be on their foreheads. And night will be no more. They will need no light of lamp or sun, for the Lord God will be their light, and they will reign forever and ever. And he said to me, 'These words are trustworthy and true . . .'" (Rev. 22:3–6)

Trustworthy and true

What a Savior! How precious is His Word!

Thank you for studying with me. I'd love to connect with you at kimjaggers.com.

For His Glory,

Kim Jaggers

About the Author

Kim Jaggers has seen God be faithful through unfathomable tragedy in her own life, detailed in her acclaimed book *Truth to Hold On To*. Because His Word sustained her when life fell apart, she has a passion for helping others know that they can truly trust Jesus more than they trust themselves and run to Him in a real daily relationship. As a speaker, writer, and ministry leader, Kim has encouraged and challenged countless others around the globe. Her writings feel like a conversation with a trusted friend. You'll find yourself laughing, crying, and loving Jesus more.

Kim Jaggers lives with her family near Knoxville, Tennessee. Find her online at kimjaggers.com, on Facebook.com/KimJaggersDailySeekingHim, and on Twitter @kim_jaggers.

Truth to Hold On To

As a young wife and mom, I had been walking with Jesus in a real relationship for just a few short years when tragedy hit.

My life became far from what I had planned or expected.

As much as I had seen God work in my life, as much as His Word encouraged me, I still found myself asking Him, "Why is my life so far different from what I had planned?" So many times I prayerfully offered up my best solutions and wondered why God had not acted in His power to make things easier for me emotionally and physically.

Some days, I would walk ahead in peace and patience, feeling God so close. Yet many days, I found my blessings harder to see, especially days when I found myself physically and emotionally drained.

The enemy tried to convince me God had forsaken me, that He had somehow sold me short or let me down. He tried to take my eyes off God's blessings to drown me in my pain.

I knew God as my Savior and faithful Father. I recognized He loved me, but honestly, sometimes, part of me wanted nothing more than to die. I knew I had blessings, but I had been angry with God for the ones I no longer had.

What's more, my life had fallen apart during a time when I had been doing my Bible study, when I had been trying to follow Jesus and be obedient, and when I had truly been worshiping Him. The enemy used even this.

I had believed the lie that if I followed God, He would make things go well for me, which I thought meant living a happy life. Like many immature churchgoers, without even saying it aloud, I had made a deal of sorts with God, and when my good behavior didn't lead to my expected results, I found myself mad at God and susceptible to believing Satan's lies.

Even though I had surrendered my life to Christ, I still idolized a life that was stable, predictable, and easy.

I had a choice to make. Would I surrender everything—even my expectations for how my life would go? I knew if I wanted lasting peace, I could not simply surrender to God on my terms; it had to be on His, and His terms might include plans for my life that would look far from how I wanted it to look.

I could continue in my anger and my bitterness, or I could dare to trust His goodness—even though I didn't understand why He had allowed everything to happen. I could hold on and dare to believe that His plans for me still included hope and a better future.

The question was, could I follow a God who does things I don't like and might do more things I don't like? Could I surrender and trust Him with my heart? Could I trust Him more than I trusted myself? Can you?

The answer has to be yes. All other choices lead to more misery and pain.

As a follower of Christ, I could not be a woman who loves God but loves my own way and my own expectations a bit more. I had to surrender all. All meant all.

God has always been in the business of bringing beauty from ashes. (Isa. 61:3) His Word is full of incredibly hopeless people finding real, stand-on, keep-going hope. His greatest miracles and supernatural peace often come in the most desperate of situations. He did this for me.

For it was there, in the midst of my greatest nightmare—before anything was fixed, in my weakest-of-weak moments—that my faithful Father helped me believe He could still do great things. And oh, He has . . . again and again.

But how? This is my story. It's not sugar-coated. It's honest. It's the times I messed up, the truth and mercy He gave, the lessons He taught—it's the *how* He carried me in the day-to-day and gave me peace to keep going. It's *Truth to Hold On To*, and I wrote it so others would know He can do the same for them.

What Others Say About
Truth to Hold On To

Loved this book — couldn't put it down! Great encouragement for anyone making it one day at a time. God is glorified!

Kim's testimony is one of hope, a hope only found in our Savior Jesus Christ. It is so amazing to me how where there is so much darkness, pain, and suffering, the light of the Gospel of Jesus shines so much brighter; there's a peace that surpasses all understanding and a never-ending hope. By reading this book, you will not only be reminded of God's faithfulness and power to save, but you will also be so convicted and so encouraged.

This is an amazing book about how one woman allowed her faith in God to grow and guide her life. She experienced trials most of us can't imagine but allowed them to point her back to our Savior. If you are struggling with life not turning out the way you hoped and need encouragement or simply want to be inspired, read this book!

Order your copy today.

Kim Jaggers has shared her story of tragedy and faith with women across the globe. Kim Jaggers' story was shared as a four-day segment on Nancy Leigh DeMoss Wolgemuth's international radio show, *Revive Our Hearts*. In addition, Kim has been a regular contributor to the *True Woman* blog and has served as a guest blogger with LifeWay's *Women Reaching Women*.

Available on KimJaggers.com and Amazon

Made in the USA
Columbia, SC
24 November 2024

47489151R00117